I'm Off To War, Mother, But I'll Be Back

Reflections of a WWII Tail Gunner

Jerry W. Whiting
and
Wayne B. Whiting

Second Edition

Edited by: Dr. Elliott S. Dushkin and LizAnn Fulgham
Front cover design by: John Streeter
                      Sheree Matousek

Book Design by Falcon Books

San Ramon, California

Paperback Edition ISBN: 978-0- 9713538-5-5
Hard bound Edition ISBN: 978-0-9713538-1-7

Library of Congress Control Number: 2007902667

Published by
Tarnaby Books
2576 Fox Circle
Walnut Creek, CA 94596

EAJWWhiting@aol.com

PRINTED IN THE UNITED STATES OF AMERICA

I dedicate this book to all the men of the 485th Bomb Group who promised their mothers they would return from the war and to the mothers, waiting anxiously, saving the letters their sons wrote, hoping and praying each letter wouldn't be the last.

Table of Contents

Acknowledgments

The author is grateful for the assistance provided by so many in the production of this book. So many stepped forward to help with the revision and it is likely I missed a few. This was not intentional. Others, not mentioned, provided encouragement and inspiration. I am particularly indebted to the Vets of the 485th Bomb Group for their assistance and to my colleagues in Europe who filled in the spaces. Some of them are listed below.

Van Anagnost

William Argie

Bonnie Bailey

Bill Baldwin

Bill Barberousse

Beulah Benshoof

Carol Bryant

John Bybee and SPG

Lynn Cotterman

Lillian Dexter

Lee Dushkin

Rose Espenshade

Bill Forsythe

Jeanne Gogolski

Edward Kapaloski family

Virgil Anderson family

Kathleen Arnold

Robert R. Baker

Everett Banker

John Beck

Bill Brokaw

Ray Bryant

Vernon O.Christensen

Hank Dahlberg

Donna Divinski

Bob Espenshade

Walter Fergus

Adam Gogolski

Robert Hickman

Tony Kujawa

Harold Kempffer

Mark Leslie

Ed McCarthy

Walter Michalke

B.W. Nauman

Waldemar Ociepski

Fabio Orlando

Bob Plocica

Maxine Rankin

Werner Schmidt

Clifford Semrau

Tony Siller

Chuck Stanley Jr.

Phil Stone

Hazen Suttkus

Greg Thompson

Barry Wareham

Doug Whiting

Orrilla Whiting

Leon Wilkins

Bill Williams

AFHRA Maxwell, Alabama

Minnehaha County Historical Society

Diane Leslie

Jackie Lyons

Sheree Matousek

Wilbur Miller

Hank O'Hagan

Dick Olson

Sherri Ortegren

Betty Ann Pratt

James A. Scheib

Sammy Schneider

Szymon Serwatka

Dan Sjodin

Fabio Stergulc

Myra Supplee

Tom Tamraz

Enzo Venci

Augusta Whiting

Lloyd Whiting

Hal Wilder

Peter Kassak

Becky Wuertemberger

Friends of Popski's Army Preservation Society

Popski's Private Army Preservation Society

Introduction

The making of this book really began during WWII, although I'm sure my dad had no idea that some very personal letters he wrote to his family would be the basis for a book more than 55 years later. Some of the stories you will read were told to me as a boy, in shortened versions.

My dad was not one of those who refused to talk about the war. For whatever reasons, he talked about it openly. I'm sure that, in his mind at least, the events of the rest of his life paled in comparison. He sanitized the more horrific parts and many of the stories he told were those of the bravery of others. His stories were also those of close friendships, trust, and respect during the last six months of the war, flying as a B-24 tail gunner with the 831st Squadron of the 485th Bomb Group, flying missions as part of the 15th Air Force over occupied Europe.

He lost track of many of his crew members and friends from the war, but he never forgot them. They lived on in his stories. He kept in touch with two close buddies from his crew after the war (B.W. Nauman and Bill Miller) and he tried to find the others. Several years ago he managed to find most of them.

Over the years I've met most of Dad's crew and, without exception, they are extraordinary people. I often thought that Dad should record some of his stories so they wouldn't be lost or forgotten, but I knew that Dad wasn't a writer and Mom had a hard time even getting him to write a note on a Christmas card. Time went on and after Bob Baker, Dad's pilot, wrote a book about his wartime experiences in Italy, I was glad that someone had recorded some of the stories.

A few years ago Dad was diagnosed with Alzheimer's disease. He and I were talking one day about getting together with some of his crew and Mom suggested that I start writing down Dad's experiences from WWII, so that they wouldn't be lost. She suggested I might be interested in the letters Dad wrote to his mother during the war. She produced a box with more than 200 letters in it, all written by Dad.

I took the letters home with me. What a treasure chest of history! After reading several, I decided to write this book. I was hopeful that the letters would tell Dad's story. The blanks would be filled in by interviews with Dad (on his good days), interviews with surviving crew members and airmen and their families, official 485th Bomb Group records, and personal diaries.

I wanted this information to be factual. There are stories Dad told me that I wanted to include and which I know are true, but I couldn't verify them. They will remain untold. I have interviewed many men from the 485th Bomb Group. They really do share a common bond, one that I can't explain. The letters are Dad's personal letters. I did the necessary research and verified the remainder of the information in this book. I also wrote the words to the stories he shared.

This started out to be the story of one airman and his experiences. As it progressed the focus shifted and it became more the story of family, a combat crew, friendships and the dedicated, brave men of the 485th Bomb Group. I know he'd prefer it that way.

Update 2007

I never imagined there would be enough interest to warrant a second edition of this book. Since the original version was released in 2001, new information has surfaced, much of it from Veterans who read the first book and provided additional first-hand descriptions of events. Dad would be thrilled to know his buddies responded. Other answers were provided by some of our friends in Europe. The careful reader will note a few minor corrections and changes, some condensation in chapters and a substantial increase in the details of a few of the events. I've also added one complete chapter of photos. Dad's story hasn't changed, though. I hope you enjoy the book.

JW

Prologue
A Time to Reflect

It was May 29th, 1945. We were getting close to U. S. soil on our last leg from Newfoundland to Bradley Field, Connecticut. I had plenty of time to think about all that we'd been through, the close calls we had, knowing that it was over….. for a while at least. The European war was over and our entire crew had survived. As I looked out a waist window, feeling the vibration of the four engines on the B-24, events of the recent past appeared.

There was the brand new plane we flew on one mission. Our pilot really liked the way it flew and thought about trying to get the plane assigned to us. After that mission the plane never flew again. The navigator counted 132 flak holes on one outer wing and the entire plane was similarly peppered with small holes. Thoughts of all that flak thrown up at us made me shudder.

Then there was the mission when we were over Klagenfurt, in southern Austria. On our way home we went through some flak and the navigator happened to be looking his side window when the Plexiglas was hit by shrapnel, penetrating it. Fortunately, his leather helmet and oxygen mask prevented him from being injured.

There was our pilot's scare on a mission over Austria when his foot was violently knocked off the rudder pedal on the bomb run. He flew the plane back safely, to find upon landing, a large flak fragment had lodged near the rudder pedal just inches from his foot.

Or the time when we were getting ready to land after a mission, low on fuel. We were circling with the formation when the pilot called the tower, requesting immediate clearance for landing. Clearance was granted and we left the formation and headed down. The assistant flight engineer was calling out the airspeed from his position behind the pilots. We had almost touched down when we apparently hit some prop wash from the plane in front of us. The right wing dipped and almost touched the runway. The copilot, always alert, pushed all four throttles to maximum power and pulled back on the controls. We shot up and went around to make another pass and land. As we were taxiing to our hardstand one of the engines quit. We'd made it home on fumes.

There was also the copilot's close call, discovered only after we got home. We had returned from a mission in *Tail Heavy* and had landed safely at Venosa when our crew chief, Sgt. Houlihan, asked the copilot if he was OK. He had no idea what Houlihan was talking about, but soon found out. Houlihan pointed to a good-sized hole in the side of the plane, alongside the copilot's position in the cockpit. They removed a .50 caliber shell casing from the insulation just inside the plane. The copilot speculated that the ball turret gunner in a plane in front of us ejected a live round from his gun as our formation climbed over the Adriatic Sea. The round hit our #3 propeller, exploding. The prop threw the casing into the side of the plane, barely missing the copilot.[1]

Hosier, the upper gunner, saved the piece of flak that came through his turret and bounced off his flak helmet on a "milk run" over northern Italy. Was that the same mission where one of my gun barrels was hit, bending it at an odd angle, the one where there were matching holes in the bottom and top of my turret? I started to sweat as the incidents began to run together in my mind. There were all those times we returned with flak holes, all those planes I'd observed going down and all those men, some of them our friends, who didn't return. It was difficult to keep the missions separated or to remember exactly when these things happened. There were also the unanswered question, "Why them and not us?"

Some things were better left in Italy. There were so many times when things could have turned out differently. We had been extremely lucky and we were now getting close to the good old USA. Yippee!

Prelude to My War

I grew up on a farm near Milbank, South Dakota. Milbank is a town about 10 miles from the Minnesota border, in northeastern South Dakota. My earliest recollection of seeing an airplane occurred when I was about 10 or 12 years old. This was in the early 1930's. I was out in the field one day and looked up to see several bombers flying north in formation. It was quite a sight to see. We later read in the newspaper that the U.S. Army Air Corps was flying a training mission to Canada. At the time I recall wondering what it would be like to fly in a big airplane, dreaming that I might get an opportunity someday.[1]

Times were not easy in South Dakota during the Depression years. I left school after the 8th grade in 1937 to help support the family. There was no high school nearby and education wasn't a priority in those times. Helping support our family was more important. I do wish I could have attended high school though. There were 11 children in our family. One of my sisters, Dorothy, died as a child, but our family was about average size in those days for a farming family.

We had no electricity on the farm. Power hadn't yet been brought to our rural region of South Dakota. There were no

1. Early Whiting family photo. Wayne is front center.

phones and we didn't have running water or indoor plumbing. We pumped our water from an outside well and seemed to get by. It was a cold trip to the outhouse in the winter, with freezing temperatures, the prairie wind blowing and snow on the ground.

The farmhouse was small, tiny by modern standards. Downstairs was the kitchen with the woodburning stove, another small room used as a bedroom by the girls, and the livingroom. Upstairs was a tiny room that was used as a bedroom for the boys. My parents slept in the livingroom. There was no insulation. In the summer when it was warm, my brothers and I slept in the barn. There was more room there. The nearby roads were gravel, at best.

I worked on our 40-acre farm and on nearby farms. There was a gravel pit on part of our 40 acres and rest of it wasn't very fertile. We were able to survive, but that was about all. We rented several acres from nearby farmers, which helped. There were some drought years that were tough on everyone. Our busiest times were in the fall, when it came time to harvest the crops. That's when I could make the most money, helping out the neighbors,

2. Wayne on left, with cousins Ivan and Don Pratt and brother Al.

many who were of German ancestry. Some of the children who were a little older than me attended the nearby German school. Many of the local farmers and their families still spoke German and it was common to hear German spoken in their homes and in the fields. While working on neighboring farms, I often slept in their barns at night, eating my meals with the families. It was hard work in the fields. It was easier on our family when the boys worked on nearby farms, because there were fewer mouths to feed.

In 1941, times were still not very good around Milbank. There wasn't much work and there was no such thing as minimum wage. There just weren't any opportunities for a young man. I decided to go to California where my Aunt Ethel lived. I heard there was plenty of work out there, with the Defense plants gearing up for the possibility of war. On December 7th, 1941, Pearl Harbor was bombed. I left the farm December 13th, hitchhiking to California, nineteen years old, with about $15 in my pocket. I was very lucky and managed to make it to Long Beach within a week, with a few dollars still in my pocket, and I moved in with my Aunt Ethel.

Within a short period of time I was able to get a job at the Douglas Aircraft Company in Long Beach. The money was very good, especially compared to the $1 per day wages working as a farm hand. There was also lots of overtime. I worked on C-47's, riveting sheet metal. The Draft was in full swing, but I had a deferment because my job was considered important to the war effort. I didn't have to worry about going into the military. For the first time in my life, I had plenty of money.

All the Defense plants were looking for workers. An older sister and her husband soon came to California for work. My parents and three younger sisters followed and Dad immediately found employment. Within just a few months, half of my immediate family was in California.

It started to bother me though, seeing all the young men in uniform. I felt they were staring at me, wondering why I wasn't in uniform. My cousin, Jamie Kimball, had gone into the Army Air Corps as a gunner and was overseas in England, serving with the 306th Bomb Group in the 8th Air Force. He had been on one of the early crews to go overseas. One other cousin, Ivan Pratt, was in the Army. The family was proud of both of them, but no one in my immediate family was in the military. I felt that I had a duty to do my part. [2]

By 1943, I couldn't just enlist because of the way the deferment program was set up. I could quit my job at Douglas and lose my deferment. I would then be drafted, but I couldn't enlist. I decided to quit, despite the protests of my supervisor. I did get drafted into the Army fairly quickly and could state a duty preference, with no certainty that I would get it. I initially considered being a paratrooper, but my mother wanted none of this. My second choice was aerial gunner, like cousin Jamie.

3. Wayne with brothers Lee, Howard and Al in Ortonville (June 1943).

I quit my job and took the train back home. I got off the train in Ortonville, Minnesota, which was about 10 miles from Milbank and spent some time with friends and the relatives who were still there. I knew I might not see them again for a long time. After a short visit I returned to California by train, to learn my draft notice had arrived.

4. Orrilla Whiting, Wayne's mother

On the 17th of July I reported to Fort MacArthur, California for induction. This wasn't very far from where I lived in Long Beach. I worked at the PX for a few days serving refreshments, while waiting to go to Basic Training. There were few restrictions at Fort MacArthur. I was issued a uniform and recall that I saw Frank Sinatra on stage one night. The uniform and shoes were several sizes too large.

August 2, 1943

Dear Mother,

I've been working at the PX where they have refreshments for the boys. It is my first time serving behind the counter. I get a kick out of it.

August 5, 1943

Dear Mother,

I sure look funny in my uniform. I don't look good at all. Tell Beulah (one of my sisters) I saw Frank Sinatra last night on stage. He sure can sing.

Within just a few days it was time to ship off to Basic Training. I was going to Florida by train. Aunt Ethel had a car, so she and my mother picked me up and drove me to the train station. The whole area around the train was roped off and there were young men everywhere, waiting to be assigned to a car and allowed to board the train. I signed in and went behind the rope. Aunt Ethel, always an independent woman, decided she wanted to say one last goodbye and pushed past the guard to get to me. She was escorted out of the roped area by the military police. It was kind of embarrassing for me. It was pretty obvious that the military wanted no lingering goodbyes.

Several days later the train arrived in Miami Beach, Florida. I was assigned to the Army Air Corps and requested to be trained as an aerial gunner, but there was no guarantee that my request would be granted. I also requested to go to Armorer School.

August 15, 1943

Dear Mother,

I am sure glad I made the Army Air Corps. I only hope I make aerial gunner so I can look forward to promotion.

Basic Training was supposed to last 48 days. It was the same as infantry basic training. The Air Force later changed to a different type, but I got the tougher, infantry-style training. I didn't mind it and I certainly got in good physical shape.

August 17, 1943

Dear Mother,

Well, I know now that I am going to school after 2 months basic training here, but I don't know where it will be. It will be either airplane mechanics, photographer, or sheet metal mechanics school. So I know where I am at now. Don't worry about me. I am fine and get plenty to eat.

August 22, 1943

Dear Mother,

We start training tomorrow on the drill field. So far, here, we just marched around the streets in Miami Beach. I like to march and guess I will get enough of it, starting tomorrow. I like to march with a band and our training group is going to have our own band. Miami Beach is where the army started the idea of singing while they marched to take the mens' minds off the work of marching in the heat.

September 1, 1943

Dear Mother,

I like the army pretty well, considering everything. Of course we have to take a lot and are under strict orders, but it isn't as bad if one can see the good points to being strict. I haven't got a real cussing out since I've been here. I seem to get along with everyone swell. Yesterday was payday for me and how much do you think I got? $8.50 for a month! Isn't that some wages!

We were shown how to pitch a tent today and also had to disassemble and assemble the Thompson sub-machine gun. That is really a gun. Our flight may get to march in the Labor Day parade if we're here then. I guess it won't be so long before I see some more of the world. The sergeant said we could be shipped out after 24 days and this is 21 days, but don't think it will be that soon.

September 6, 1943

Dear Mother,

Well, I am so tired I am nearly ready to drop. This afternoon we had physical training period and they ran us around the field 4 times and we couldn't stop unless we passed out, and the field is about 2 miles around it. Today was really hot and our toughest day of training. They will either make good physically trained soldiers out of us or kill us, by the way it looks. We also had assembly and disassembly of the .30 caliber U.S. carbine gun today. I will be glad when my basic training is through.

September 26, 1943

Dear Mother,

Well, about me going into combat, don't worry about it, as they no doubt will give me more training. I went and took another test, for aerial gunner, yesterday and I qualified. So if they have any openings in gunnery school they will send me to one. A lieutenant gave a speech yesterday and told us we are subject to being moved any day now. So, for the married he said they shouldn't have their wives come down here, as we could leave any day. He said, for the ones who feared they would be sent across (overseas) from here, don't worry, as it would be very unfortunate if they were shipped overseas right from here, although it has happened.

There were various times in training that rumors circulated about finishing early and sending the troops directly into combat. I heard these rumors at nearly every training school I attended. It may have happened to some, but it didn't happen to me.

October 23, 1943

Dear Mother,

Well I just got back from classification and found out what I will be. They had me down as sheet metal mechanics school and not qualified as an aerial gunner. I asked them why I wasn't (qualified) and they said they didn't know. So I went over and talked to the combat crew sergeant and he said "do you want gunner?" and I told him yes, so he signed me up for it and called up headquarters and told them to put me down as aerial gunner.....also armorer. If I am not shipped overseas when I complete this training I will be sent to aircraft mechanics crew schooling.

NOTES AND REFERENCES

1 In July and August of 1934 Lt. Colonel Hap Arnold led a flight of ten B-10 bombers from Bolling Field, near Washington D.C., to Fairbanks, Alaska and back. This was a display of airpower, for which Arnold received the Distinguished Flying Cross. He also received the Mackay Trophy, an award for aeronautical achievement. Arnold was commander of the Army Air Forces during WWII. Undoubtedly this is the flight Wayne witnessed as an 11 year-old boy.

2 Two brothers failed the army physical exam and the oldest brother was in his early 30's, married, with several children, and was deferred. There were two other cousins in Wisconsin who were in the army, but none of the other nearby relatives were serving. The family had a long history of military service, dating before the Revolutionary War.

Advanced Training

At the end of October I boarded a troop train in Miami, destination Denver, Colorado. A few of the guys from Basic Training were on the train with me. One was Billy Barberousse and we quickly became good friends. We were only let off the train twice, briefly, for exercise.

We arrived in Denver in the middle of the night. It was freezing and all I was wearing was a summer uniform. Late October weather in Denver is a lot different than Miami weather. Armament School was at Buckley Field. Denver was a nice place to be and the people were very friendly. Here I learned about the guns, the operation of the various bomber turrets, the bomb release mechanisms, and other things related to armament on bombers. This training would last about 4 months.

November 28, 1943

Dear Mother,

We saw a picture of aerial gunners in certain past raids. Sure looks exciting. Can't wait 'til I get my first ride in a plane.

Billy Barberousse and I spent a lot of our free time together. He was from Oklahoma and we seemed to have a lot in common. Denver didn't seem like a big city to us. We toured Denver on bicycles and tried not to miss too many weekend dances.

January 11, 1944

Dear Mother,

I am working on the synchronizing of the guns to shoot between the propeller (blades) without shooting them off. It is really tricky work.

January 25, 1944

Dear Mother,

I heard a rumor that we only have 2 weeks of school left. I heard another rumor that we may go over to England or Australia, for our gunner schooling, but these are more or less latrine rumors, as we call them. I got to run a turret today for 15 minutes. I sure like it. It takes quite a bit of thinking and coordination to keep the sight on the targets while moving the turret.

January 28, 1944

Dear Mother,

I like turrets and the instructions in them. We have had the Consolidated turret, the Martin turret and started this morning on the Sperry ball turret, used underneath the B-17. I ran one for about 1/2 hour today on the ground and I will take the ball turret if I should have my choice.

As training neared completion, I had mixed feelings about leaving Denver. The people were so nice here. It wasn't unusual for families to invite servicemen into their homes on weekends, often for Sunday dinner. In those days Denver was a very friendly place to be.

March 1, 1944

Dear Mother,

As you know I am leaving Buckley. Don't know for sure, but am positive I will end up at Tyndall Field (Florida)....anyway, I am going to Gunnery School. I just packed my barracks bag and will be all set to leave tonight at 5:30.

Often our orders didn't include our destination. Rumors circulated about where we might be going and often, stateside at least, the rumors were correct. I had a chance to stay at Buckley, as an instructor. The atmosphere in Denver was wonderful, but I felt it was time to move on, and the troop train did take me to Tyndall Field for Gunnery School. Billy Barberousse got sick before we left, so he stayed in Denver. I moved on to Florida without my buddy.[1]

Any serviceman who has ever ridden on troop trains knows how boring and uncomfortable this form of travel is. At some stops we weren't allowed off the train at all, and at others we could briefly get off for exercise. The trains were always packed with troops going somewhere, or returning from somewhere. I was anxious for my train ride to end and also anxious to begin gunnery school.

March 29, 1944

Dear Mother,

I will answer that question why I didn't want to stay at Denver as an instructor. I want to be a gunner and do something. If I hadn't wanted to fight for my country I wouldn't have come in here (the Air Force).

I enjoyed gunnery school. It was nice being back in the warm Florida climate. I was a pretty good shot, but I became much better. I enjoyed skeet shooting. I had a problem at first with being nervous, but an instructor spent some time with me and I learned to relax. I eventually hit 25 out of 25 on the skeet range, which was pretty good for a country boy.

We progressed to the moving range, where we were driven around a course, standing on a platform on the back of a truck. There were skeet houses, separated by about 40-50 yards. As we were driven through the mile-long course, clay pigeons came out of the skeet houses in all different directions. It kept us pretty busy, learning to shoot at them, but it was a lot of fun.

We spent a lot of time with the .50 caliber machine gun. We learned to assemble it and disassemble it in the dark. We were tested at various phases in our training. Our instructors would put a broken part in the gun and we learned to quickly find, remove and replace the broken part.

Prior to our air-to-air training, we fired machine guns at a cloth target which was mounted on the back of a Jeep and towed around a circular course. The bullets had been dipped in various paint colors, so the instructors could tell our individual scores by the paint transfer on the cloth targets. It was only near the end of our training that we got a chance to fly.

April 23, 1944

Dear Mother,

We went out yesterday on our first training mission. It sure was grand. We stayed up 3 1/2 hours. There are 8 students, 3 instructors, and pilot and copilot in one B-17. It liked it very much, except I ain't got used to the oxygen mask. The best feeling I had was when we rose off the ground.

During the aerial portion of our training we often fired at cloth targets towed behind a single-engine AT-6 trainer. Fortunately, we didn't hit the trainer, or at least we weren't told about it. Hits on the target were again scored by checking the paint transfer marks on the target. I had fun and my time at the school passed quickly.

5. Wayne with youngest sister Donna while home on leave (May 27, 1944).

May 6, 1944

Dear Mother,

This morning we attended graduation exercises....the whole class of 44-10. We had to go up and salute the officer and he presented us with our silver wings. I am a corporal, starting today. I am on shipping orders, I think for AAF Lincoln, Nebraska. There are just 28 of us going, all armorer/gunners.

I left Tyndall on May 9th, by train again, and arrived in Lincoln on the 11th. Almost immediately I got a 15-day leave, so I was able to get back to Long Beach to visit my parents. It was another long train trip, something to which I was becoming accustomed. It was well worth the trip, because I believed I would be going overseas soon and would probably not get another chance to visit them. After a visit with them, I boarded a train for another long ride back to Nebraska.

When I arrived back in Lincoln at the end of May, I was disappointed to learn I would not be continuing my training there, since it was only a few hundred miles from my home. Lincoln was only to be an assignment center for me, but I hoped I would get to meet my crew there.

June 12, 1944

Dear Mother,

I got my crew number, which is 6266 and this morning I went up to the officers' quarters and got the names of three officers who are crewed up with me. They changed things here lately. The officers don't get to pick their crew. My officers haven't come to see me yet, but they usually do see their gunners before they leave here.

As it turned out, I didn't get to meet my officers at Lincoln. It was rumored that we would be going to Boise, Idaho, for operational training. I knew I'd be flying in the B-24 Liberator, the plane that became famous for the Ploesti raid in 1943.

June 13, 1944

Dear Mother,

I am leaving in the morning at 10 o'clock. They won't tell us where we are going, but we all think we are going to Boise, Idaho.

June 16, 1944

Dear Mother,

Here I am at Boise. I met the whole crew tonight, the three officers—the first pilot and copilot and bombardier and my flight engineer and assistant and radio man, and the two career gunners. I seem to like every one of them from sight and guess I will, anyway, as we are going through this thing together. My first pilot seems like a swell Joe. He's the boy I have to satisfy. He's my commanding officer now.

We finally began our training as a crew at Gowen Field, Boise, Idaho. Bob Baker was our pilot. He seemed quiet and very serious-minded, just the right person for the job. Bob was from Battle Creek, Michigan. We learned that his father was a minister. Bob was a non-drinker, something that was unusual at the time for a young man. His non-drinking status later became a benefit for me, when we flew combat missions. He gave me his after-mission ration of whiskey, which I saved for a special occasion. Bob was recently married and his wife Jeanette joined us at Boise.

Jim Scheib was our copilot. He was one of the youngest men on the crew and had just turned 20. Jim wanted to be a fighter pilot, but the needs of the military came first, and he was assigned to our crew. Jim was an excellent pilot. He was from Pittsburgh, Pennsylvania and single.

Richard McLawhorn was our bombardier. He was a good-natured man from Greenville, North Carolina and married. His wife and baby boy joined him at Boise. As the armorer/gunner, I interacted a lot with Mac. My responsibilities included helping the bombardier arm the bombs on combat missions.

Hazen Suttkus, our navigator, joined the crew after we began training. Hazen was married and was originally from Ohio. More recently he resided in southern California, where he worked at Douglas Aircraft in Santa Monica. Hazen was very efficient and business-like. He was one of the older members of our crew, second only to our radio operator/waist gunner, Bill Miller.

Bill Miller was the "old man" of the crew at 28. I'd have to say that Bill was more mature than most of us enlisted men. There where several occasions where he kept me in line, for which I'm still grateful. Bill was single and from Illinois. As time went on, I became good friends with Bill. He was responsible for operating the air-to-ground radios and maintaining our airborne communications. On later combat missions, Bill also operated "Panther", a device designed to jam the radar of the anti-aircraft batteries that were shooting at us.

B.W. Nauman was our flight engineer/waist gunner. B.W. was from Rockport, Missouri and came from a farming background, much like my own. He got married while we were at Gowen Field. I was in the hospital with pneumonia at the time, so I couldn't attend his wedding. B.W. had more flying experience than the rest of us gunners. He had previously flown on antisubmarine patrols off the East Coast. B.W. was pretty busy when we flew combat. As the flight engineer, he was kept occupied before the missions, working with the ground mechanics and making sure the engines were tuned up and functioning properly. During the missions he had a lot of additional responsibilities, such as transferring fuel and troubleshooting any engine or mechanical problems that might arise. B.W. and I had very similar backgrounds and we became good friends, spending much of our time together while overseas.

Bill Argie, from New York, was our ball turret gunner and assistant flight engineer. He was single and fairly short, like me, but had a more muscular build. After Bill entered his turret on each mission, we'd crank it down into position beneath the plane.

6. Bob Baker crew photo, taken during the summer of 1944. Front (L-R) Richard McLawhorn, bombardier; James Scheib, copilot; Hazen Suttkus, navigator and Robert Baker, pilot. Back (L-R) John Manfrida, nose gunner; Bill Miller, radio operator/waist gunner; Fred Hosier, upper turret gunner; William Argie, ball gunner; Wayne Whiting, tail gunner and B.W. Nauman, flight engineer/waist gunner.

Fred Hosier was our upper turret gunner and a "career gunner", meaning he had no additional assignment on the plane, except as a gunner. Fred was married and from New York. His wife joined him at Boise. Fred was a tall, thin man and claimed to have been a rumrunner in years past.

John Manfrida, another "career gunner", was our nose turret gunner. John was another New Yorker. He was a broad-shouldered man, quiet most of the time, and started out to be a military policeman before becoming an aerial gunner. ·

I was assigned as the tail gunner. I don't recall exactly how the assignment was made, but I believe I was given my choice of positions, since I was the armorer/gunner. We began flying training missions together and rapidly became a team. I began spending a lot of time in the tail turret and soon learned I was prone to airsickness. This malady would also plague me in combat and I was never able to rid myself of the problem.

We soon learned that even non-combat flying could be dangerous. A B-24 crashed and exploded one night when returning from a training mission.

July 2, 1944

Dear Mother,

I wrote about a plane being afire the other night. It had caught fire in midair and crash-landed. Three of the crew bailed out and the other eight men were killed….. The plane was 0019. We landed at 6:40 that night in that plane. It happened about 9:15 PM.

July 6, 1944

Dear Mother,

We've really got a good bombardier. We were flying at 16,000 feet and he dropped a bomb 20' from the dead center of the target.

We had a lot of gunnery and bombing practice. During the in-flight gunnery practice, we fired on targets that were towed by other planes. These targets would approach us from different positions and we practiced calling out the location of the "attacks" and shooting at the targets. We also practiced low-level air-to-ground gunnery, where we'd shoot at stationary targets on the ground from our turrets. The pilot also had all of us try to fly the plane, with his assistance, of course. That was quite an experience. I was given my chance in the cockpit when we flew a long-range flight to San Francisco and back, near the end of our training.

July 31, 1944

Dear Mother,

I was in the copilot seat helping the pilot fly Saturday for two hours. I sure liked it. I just found out today that our pilot is a preacher's son. No wonder he doesn't cuss much. Ha! Ha!

During the first week of August we completed our training. We had a crew party to celebrate the occasion. We had no idea where we'd be sent. At the time, the war in Europe was going well. Rumors were rampant and various airmen had "inside sources" with a wide variety of potential destinations for us.

August 4, 1944

Dear Mother,

We had our crew party last night. We had a swell time at the party. Lt. Baker and wife, Lt. McLawhorn and wife and baby boy, Flight Officer Suttkus and wife, Lt. Scheib, Sgt. Nauman and wife, Corporal Hosier and wife, Corporal Miller, Corporal Manfrida, Corporal Argie and myself were there. I think the biggest part of the bombing runs will be done in Europe by the 1st of September. My guess to our overseas station is CBI (China Burma India).

How wrong I was about the war being nearly finished in Europe. It must have been wishful thinking. On completion of our training, we received orders to report to Topeka, Kansas. After all our training together, I felt confident that we were ready for combat. We had several days to get to Topeka, so I was able to make a quick side trip to visit my relatives in South Dakota and Minnesota. From there I went by train to Topeka, where I met up with my crew. We were soon put on a troop train, destination Newport News, Virginia. We were not told what our overseas destination would be.

NOTES AND REFERENCES

1 Billy Barberousse ended up as a gunner on a B-25 in the Pacific. He and Wayne wrote to each other while overseas but, after a few months, Barberousse's letters came were returned. Wayne assumed he had been killed, but this was not the case. His group was island-hopping and Barberousse's mail didn't catch up to him.

Destination Italy

On September 11th, we boarded the *Richard J. Gatling,* a Liberty ship, destination…..somewhere overseas. We left port and were two days out to sea when there was a problem with the engine and we returned to port. We were given a couple of days leave while the ship was repaired. Some of us went to see Washington D.C. and I got to see the sights there, the Smithsonian Institute being the highlight of my trip. We returned to Newport News, where we again boarded the *Richard J. Gatling* on September 21st, for what was to be a 26-day journey to Italy.

The trip overseas wasn't as bad as it could have been. None of our crew got seasick. We were packed into the ship like sardines. Our bunks were canvas and stacked several high. It was certainly not a cruise ship. The bunks for the enlisted men of our crew were in the bottom of the forward hold, so we tried to get up on deck whenever possible for fresh air. We caught up to a large convoy that left port ahead of us and there were ships as far as one could see.

At the end of our first week we got our first shower, a salt water shower. It left us feeling sticky, but it was still better than

7. "Tough guys" aboard ship. (L-R: Bill Argie, B.W. Nauman and Bill Miller)

nothing. Most of us grew beards, because it was difficult to shave with cold salt water. Some of the gunners, myself included, got a little relief from the boredom by being trained to operate the 20 millimeter anti-aircraft guns on deck. We still had a lot of free time. Some of us played cards or rolled dice to pass the time.

Some of us were playing poker one day and I began to win. I wasn't a good poker player but I started winning. Manfrida got mad at me. I don't know if he was just a poor sport, if we'd been aboard the ship too long, or if I'd said something that upset him. For whatever reason, he accused me of cheating. He jumped up and started to come in my direction. Miller, always the calming influence, stepped between us. Needless to say, that was the end of the card game. We stayed away from each other for a while, but we always got along fine after that. I just didn't play cards with him. In retrospect, I think the cramped quarters and boredom got to us all a little bit.

October 7, 1944

Dear Mother,

There isn't much to write about, but will drop you a line to have something to do. I am sure tired of lying around but guess I will be busier in the near future. Guess you know I will be somewhere in Italy when you receive this.

Several days out to sea we were told our destination was Italy. At last we knew where we were going. There was all sorts of speculation before our destination was announced, but most thought we were headed for England, Italy, or the China-Burma-India Theater. It seemed like the trip took forever. We could only go as fast as the slowest ship in the convoy and we zigzagged all the way across the Atlantic in order to protect ourselves from submarine attack. We were told that our convoy averaged about 10 miles per hour.

October 10, 1944

Dear Mother,

I will drop you a few lines today as I am just lying around again. I have been playing cards to pass the time away. We have come through the Straits of Gibraltar and saw the rock quite plain. It looked as it does in all the pictures. This voyage seems like a voyage such as Columbus made, although we know we will hit land someday and he didn't. I never dreamed there was so much water in the Atlantic Ocean. Of course we are in the Mediterranean now.

After 18 days we entered the Mediterranean Sea and finally landed at Naples on October 16th, after a 26-day voyage. As the ship prepared to come into port, small Italian fishing boats pulled alongside. Money was sent up from the fishing boats, tied to a rope. The Red Cross representative lowered cigarettes over the side of the ship after getting the money. This was my first taste of the Black Market in Italy. It left me with a sick feeling to think that

Red Cross cigarettes, intended for the GIs, were being sold in this fashion. The Red Cross did a lot of good things for servicemen, but I never forgot this one incident.

We pulled alongside the partially sunken, overturned hull of a ship, our first sign of the destruction which we would soon experience firsthand. The hull of the ship was above water and our gangplank was lowered over the hull. When our turn came, we walked down the gangplank, onto the side of the overturned hull and onto shore.

We were taken by truck to the 19th Replacement Depot, about 15 miles north of Naples, near a town called Martinese. The truck ride took us through the streets of Naples. It was a dirty, smelly, war-torn city, which left a lasting impression on all of us. The people we saw looked dirty and poor. Small children were wandering the streets and many looked homeless. We were glad to be on land again, but uncertain about our future. We were getting closer to the war for which we had prepared.

We stayed at the Replacement Depot for a few days, taking a few walking tours of the area, visiting the Red Cross, and generally waiting for the next step. We still didn't know exactly where we were headed in Italy or to which bomb group we'd be assigned.

October 20, 1944

Dear Mother,

I expect to do my part here. This coming over here wasn't a wish, but my duty for my country I love. I am writing this by candlelight and it's rather hard to see.

One morning, further orders arrived and we boarded an Italian version of a troop train. We were assigned to a boxcar, which had straw covering the floor. We were given K rations and a supply of water, and the train slowly got under way. It was a very slow train and it seemed that one could easily jog just as fast as the train. At times we pulled off onto sidings. Some of the men raided nearby grape vineyards, but the grapes tasted sour. We were traveling east through the Italian countryside and we spent the night on the train. Our final destination turned out to be Gioia, where we arrived October 21st.

Some of the crew got mail at Gioia and we spent the night there. Several of the enlisted men went to have a few drinks at the Enlisted Men's Club. Gioia was an actual airbase and there were B-24's based there, so we felt more comfortable. Things also seemed a little more orderly. Here we were given our assignment to the 485th Bomb Group. On October 22nd, a B-24 picked us up and flew us to Venosa, home of the 485th. The flight was short, lasting about 30 minutes. On arrival, we were assigned to the 831st Squadron, one of four squadrons in the 485th. The other squadrons were the 828th, 829th and 830th. We arrived about 5:00PM, while it was still light.

The four officers from our crew were assigned a tent and the six enlisted men were assigned another tent. Our tent was cold. There were no available cots or bunks that night, so we had to scavenge. The enlisted men found some large boxes to take to our tent. I swear these boxes were coffins, but some of the other men said they were boxes that the fins for the bombs were packed in. It rained the next day and the tent badly leaked. We tried to waterproof the tent with tar and stopped many of the major leaks.

October 24, 1944

Dear Mother,

I expect you are wondering where I am by now. Well I am somewhere in Italy. Things are rather strange here, but one will get used to them I expect. Living conditions for the GI aren't as bad as I thought they would be, but can't say they are sweet. I had a drink of gin last night and it tasted like 100 octane gasoline. I got my six cans of beer today, a weeks ration.

We began improvising, since we correctly assumed this tent would be home for the duration of the European war. One of the first things we needed was a heat source, since the weather was already cold. (We were issued cots shortly after our arrival.) We met other crews and saw that stoves were being built from 55-gallon oil drums. This became a priority for us. We built our own stove similar to those in neighboring tents.

The fuel storage tank was a 55-gallon oil drum or a drop tank (auxiliary gasoline tank) from a fighter plane, placed on a stand outside the tent. We ran a metal fuel line from the storage tank, inside the tent along the floor, to a half-drum (55-gallon oil drum cut in half), placed on tufa blocks, in the center of the tent. [1] A clamp or petcock was placed on the line before it entered the half-drum, as a fuel shut-off and regulator. For a chimney, we used German 88-millimeter shell casings. We cut off the ends of the casings and stacked them on top of one another, out the ceiling of our tent. The bottom end was placed in a hole on top of the stove.

After the stove was finished, we put 100-octane aviation gas in the storage tank, slowly turned the petcock to get a drip going, and inserted a match in our stove to light it. Our homemade heat source worked fairly well. Occasionally we'd hear small explosions from other tents when the men lit their stoves and the fuel wasn't regulated properly. A few tents blew up from the homemade stoves.

This stove put out good heat and it kept our tent bearable on the coldest nights. It probably wasn't the safest way to keep warm, but we were happy to have it. Shortly after our arrival, we realized that we needed a floor covering. Many crews obtained steel runway matting for their floor and covered it with straw mats. This was called Pierced Steel Planking (PSP) or "Marston Mat". It was made of interlocking panels that could be assembled quickly. Each panel was about 10 feet long, 15 inches wide and weighed about 66 pounds. Panels could be locked together to form a tent floor, or a runway for our B-24's, which was their intended use. When covered with a straw mat, this made a pretty decent floor. We decided we wanted something a little more up-scale than a steel floor.

There was new construction going on in the area and tufa blocks were used for various construction projects. We thought these would make a good, solid floor, so we began "procuring" these blocks. After dinner each evening at the mess hall, each enlisted crew member would pick up a tufa block on the way back to our tent. Soon we had one of the best tent floors available.

October 25, 1944

Dear Mother,

We, the other enlisted men and I, are living in the same tent and several nights ago it rained hard and our tent leaked like a sieve and we nearly drowned. So today we got to work and put top dressing on it. I don't expect it will stop it entirely, but it may help. We also rigged up a gas stove and it works fairly well, for homemade. We are trying to fix up the tent as much as possible as this will be our home 'til we get back to the states. I just got back from filling our canteens with water. Well, so much for our living conditions. As you can see they aren't too good, but we'll get by. Haven't started my missions yet, but hope to get started soon. I am just fine and can't complain too much. But as my old Commanding Officer, Killer Kane, from Gowen used to say, "A good soldier has to complain a lot".[2]

The 485th had flown its first mission in early May of 1944. The group had been to all the rough targets (and they could all be rough) like Vienna, Ploesti, Regensburg, Munich and Blechhammer. Most of the original crews who survived their missions had already gone home. As we were soon to observe, many of our crews would go down over enemy territory. We only hoped they were captured and not killed.

8. Colonel John Tomhave

During my first few days at the base I looked around for familiar faces. There were one or two gunners that I'd trained with in the states. There was also one crew in our squadron that trained with us in Boise, Lt. Ken Wydler's crew, so I knew a few people.

We were anxious to learn about combat from those who had experienced it, so we talked to other experienced gunners whenever we had the opportunity. Even though most of the crews by this time were replacement crews, many of them had been at Venosa for months. Although these guys were our age or younger, many of them looked tired and much older than us. It was clear this was going to be no picnic. Most of the men hadn't been

9. Colonel "Pop" Arnold

attacked by fighters on their recent missions, but flak, weather, and mid-air crashes had taken their toll on the group. As we'd learn very quickly, this would continue to be the case throughout the remainder of our war.

Our commanding officer was Colonel John Tomhave. The original C.O., Colonel Walter "Pop" Arnold, had been shot down over Blechhammer, Germany, in August. The original squadron commander, Lt. Colonel Dan Sjodin, was still at Venosa when we arrived, but soon completed his missions and returned home.

When we ventured out to the flight line, we saw that nearly all the bombers had sustained some sort of battle damage and had

10. Lt. Colonel Daniel Sjodin

been repaired with patches of aluminum riveted to the skin of the airplanes. Most of the bombers were silver, the natural metal finish of B-24's, but there were still several of the older, olive drab B-24H's and G's in service. These were the original planes that had been there from the beginning, a few months earlier. Although they had been in service less than six months, they looked old and worn out, with silver patches covering much of the original olive drab.

It seemed like the ground crews were always working on the planes, preparing them for the next mission. They'd be there early in the morning, long before dawn. They'd be there in the afternoon, when the crews brought the planes back from missions, and they'd often work long into the night. They were a hardworking bunch of men. Unlike the flight crews, they were there for the duration of the war. If we finished our missions, we got to go home. They were never finished.

A few days after we arrived, Nauman and I went to mail call. This was always something we looked forward to. Mail was about the only link we had with home, aside from an occasional magazine or newsreel. We stood there, waiting for our names to be called. As name after name was called, someone would call out "He went down". Nearly all the names called got the same response. It made me sick. Besides, I got no mail. As we walked back to our tent, Nauman and I were a couple of sad sacks. I know what both of us were thinking, but we didn't say anything. It looked like 70-80% of the squadron had been lost. It seemed impossible that we would survive this war.

We later learned the mail that night was from several months ago that had been misplaced, or for some reason hadn't made it to the squadron. On April 20, 1944, the Liberty Ship *S.S. Paul Hamilton* was sunk by the Germans. Among its passengers were 154 men from the 485th Bomb Group, most of them from the 831st Squadron. This occurred off the coast of Algeria, during an aerial torpedo attack by a JU-88, and there were no survivors. Most of the mail that night was for these men. When we heard this, it made us feel that our chances for survival were better, but we would become accustomed to hearing "He went down" at mail call, and heard it all too frequently as our war progressed. It was even worse when the names called were our buddies.

NOTES AND REFERENCES

1 Reddish brown blocks shaped from soft, local volcanic stone

2 Colonel John "Killer" Kane was famous for leading one of the bomb groups on the low-level Ploesti raid in August 1943.

Our Entry to War

T he weather remained poor throughout the remainder of October. We flew a practice mission on October 27th, practicing formation flying over southern Italy. After our return, a couple of us checked the mission board for the next day. I saw that our crew, except for the pilot, was scheduled to fly with Lt. Blood, a pilot in the squadron who already had combat experience. Our pilot would fly his first mission with another experienced crew.

As we were standing by the mission board, one of our crew asked me if I'd heard anything about Lt. Blood. I actually hadn't, but I wouldn't admit that, and I was disappointed that our entire crew wasn't flying together. At any rate I answered, "I heard he's kinda chickenshit". I had no sooner finished my comment when I was spun around by a large hand that firmly gripped my shoulder. I found myself facing a tall 1st lieutenant, sporting a handlebar mustache. This lieutenant, who immediately identified himself as Lt. Blood, demanded to know my name and position on the bomber. I told him I was the tail gunner and armorer/gunner. With a Texas drawl, he firmly told me that he expected me to have all the guns ready for the mission and said he'd take care of flying the plane. A quick answer of "yes sir" was all I had time for, before he turned and stalked away. I hadn't learned to keep my mouth shut, but he didn't take it any further.

On October 28th, the mission was scrubbed due to bad weather, but on October 29th we were again scheduled to fly with Lt. Blood. With some apprehension we prepared for the mission. I'm not sure whether I was more apprehensive about going into combat for the first time, or of the thought of having to face Lt. Blood again. The target was Augsburg, Germany.

We took off, circling to form up with the other two planes in our element, then formed up with our box, then with our group, and headed north over the Adriatic Sea, flying a silver B-24J. We reached northern Yugoslavia before the mission was canceled, due to bad weather in the target area. We returned after five hours. We weren't attacked by fighters and didn't receive any flak, but we also didn't get any credit for the mission. I kept a pretty low profile and stayed away from Lt. Blood. I was fortunate to be in the rear of the plane. In December I would sadly watch as Lt. Blood's plane went down over Yugoslavia.

October 29, 1944

Dear Mother,

I see we have a big day ahead of us. I think I will be over here a long while the way things are going now. I have twice as many missions to put in as (cousin) Jamie had and they aren't so easy, either, from what I gather. Boy, I sure wish this war would end. I should have high morale tonight after receiving that card, but several others in my crew and I are disgusted tonight. We started our first combat mission to-day, but had to turn back on account of weather, so still got my limit to go.

My cousin, Jamie Kimball, had completed his combat tour in B-17's with the 8th Air Force in England and had been safely back in the United States for several months. At the time he completed his tour, 25 missions constituted a complete tour. I'd finally received a card from my mother, some of the first mail I received in Italy.

We flew another practice mission at the end of the month and continued to make improvements to our tent. Even the experienced crews flew very few missions in October, due to the bad weather. On November 1st, an entire crew that had completed their missions was lost when their plane blew up soon after take-off. The word got around to the different squadrons and rumors began to surface that sabotage was involved. I doubt if this was the case, since we heard no more about it.[1]

November 2, 1944

Dear Mother,

I intended to write for the past two nights, but we didn't have any candles, so I couldn't write. Our engineer and pilot flew their first combat mission yesterday, but they flew with other crews. I guess it won't be very long now before we go as a crew. Of course, the way I look at it, the sooner we get started the quicker we will get back to the states if everything goes OK. Of course it will take us longer to get our quota of missions in than it would have in the summer as the weather, I guess, won't be so good from now on. But we will make it OK, I guess. It rains about every other day here so it is always very muddy and sloppy.

We built an addition onto our tent yesterday and also tried to put light wires in the tent, but couldn't find a socket for the bulb. I washed my socks this morning in my helmet. I just sent my other washing out with an Italian. I hear they do pretty good work in washing, so will let them do it if everything works out. I hear they charge you two packages of cigarettes and I will give him two packs of those I bought on the boat for 4 cents a pack.

On November 3rd, we checked the board and saw we were scheduled to fly as a complete crew the next day. That meant

retiring early for all of us and no late night drinking at the Enlisted Men's Club. We were awakened around 3:30AM. We got
up, using a flashlight or candle to see what we were doing. There
wasn't much cleaning up to do, since we didn't have running water in our tent. A little water from my canteen in my steel helmet
served as a wash basin.

We had about 30 minutes to get to breakfast, served in the
Mess building. The breakfast menu wasn't much, but the cooks
didn't have much to work with. Powdered milk and powdered
eggs were usually available, along with toast. We never had fresh
milk or fresh eggs. The coffee wasn't too bad. I didn't feel much
like eating breakfast, so the menu didn't bother me much.

After breakfast we went to briefing. There was a curtain over
the map in the briefing building, so we couldn't see our mission
destination before the briefing started. An officer led the briefing.
When everyone was seated the briefing began and the Intelligence Officer pulled the curtain off the map and we could see
where we were going. Depending on our destination, a varied
amount of groans could be heard. Our target was Linz, Austria, a
benzol plant. Strips of ribbons were attached to the map, between
Venosa and Linz, identifying the routes to and from the target.
We were told what type of fighters would escort us and were
briefed that we'd be flying with the rest of the 55th Bomb Wing,
and ours would be the last group in formation. Information was
given about suspected flak locations and intensity, and the potential for fighter opposition. After a brief question and answer period, watches were synchronized. The gunners were dismissed,
after a prayer by Chaplain Golder, our group chaplain, and the officers remained in groups to obtain additional information.

We picked up our flight gear and headed for the flight line. A
truck picked us up and took us to our assigned bomber, which
was one of the old, olive drab B-24H's, parked on a hardstand of
Pierced Steel Planking. I don't recall which of the old bombers we
flew that day, but it was possibly *Tail Heavy*. As a new crew, we

had no choice in the matter. We arrived as the engines were being run up by the crew chief and a mechanic. After warm-up, the engines were shut down. Nauman, the flight engineer, discussed the plane's condition with the crew chief.

I threw my bag, with my parachute and other gear in it, up into the back of the plane, through the rear escape hatch. As Armorer/Gunner, I checked the fuses on the bombs to insure that the fuses were in and that the arming pins were inserted properly. McLawhorn, the bombardier, would also check this again when he and the others arrived. I also checked the turret guns and ammunition.

We all climbed into the plane to wait. My take-off position was in the waist of the plane, with several other gunners. Now was the time to wait, and worry. We finally saw a white flare near the control tower, the signal for engines to start. The auxiliary gasoline generator, or "putt-putt" as we called it, was used to start the #3 engine. One by one, the other engines were started, accompanied by backfires. After all engines were running, they were individually run at high R.P.M's. When the pilots were satisfied that everything was operating properly, Baker signaled the crew chief to remove the chocks from the wheels. The plane slowly began to move and we started our taxi, taking our place in line behind other bombers on the muddy, unpaved taxi strip.

All our bombers had a letter painted on the side of the plane, behind the waist opening. One could tell the squadron by the color of the letter. My squadron, the 831st, had blue letters. The 830th squadron had white letters, the 829th had yellow letters and the 828th had red letters. This helped us identify the other squadrons in the air. On the radio, each squadron had a call sign. Our squadron's call sign was "Rubdown". The 830th's was "Soonup". The 829th used "Wetrag" and the 828th used "Springgreen". If we were flying "Blue C", which would later be our assigned ship, our call sign would be "Rubdown C for Charlie". The call sign for our base tower was "Lightweight Tower".

I felt glad to be starting my missions with our entire crew, but I was naturally apprehensive about what to expect. Our trip to northern Yugoslavia with Lt. Blood had been uneventful, but we didn't get very far into enemy territory on that journey. I looked over at Argie, who was looking out a waist window. He looked pretty serious. There was no laughing or teasing this morning. We were headed for combat.

Our turn finally came in the line of 36 bombers. The pilots applied the brakes, then ran up the engines. As the brakes were released, the plane began to move. The plane lumbered along, slowly at first, and we felt the bumps in the steel matting of the runway. The plane gradually gathered speed. We had a full load of fuel and 500 lb. bombs, so it seemed to take forever to get our speed up. Near the end of the runway the pilots finally pulled the big bomber off the ground. As soon as we were off the ground, the landing gear was retracted. We joined up with other bombers from our group. About an hour later we joined up with the other three bomb groups in our bomb wing. Our group was the last in formation and would be the last group over the target.

We headed north and I saw several fighters in the distance. As they flew off to the side and weaved above us, I could see they were twin-tailed P-38 Lightning fighters, which would be escorting us to the target. The twin booms made them easy to identify. They were still careful not to point their noses at us as they zoomed above our formation. Pointing their noses at us was considered an act of aggression and may have caused some trigger-happy gunners to shoot at them. They were a welcome sight, especially on this first mission, when we didn't know what sort of enemy fighter opposition to expect. There were 25-35 of them.

As we headed north, ten of our B-24's left the formation at different times, all returning to base with mechanical problems. We continued to climb and the pilot told us it was time to man our guns. As we approached enemy territory, he gave the word to put on our oxygen masks. Nauman and I helped Argie get into the ball turret and then lowered the turret. I crawled into the tail turret, leaving my parachute just outside the turret in the fuselage. I carried a chest chute, which I could snap on quickly if we had to bail out. I always tried to keep it within reach.

I donned the flak vest after getting into the turret. On later missions I would take an extra flak vest or two to sit on, after realizing the main threat of flak came from below. I was wearing my Mae West life jacket beneath my parachute harness and carried my .45 automatic pistol in my coat pocket. I tied a pair of shoes to my parachute. We heard from other crews that the jolt of a parachute opening often separated an airman from his boots, so it was common practice to carry shoes in this fashion.

I didn't close the doors to my turret. I heard stories about the doors freezing shut or jamming after being hit by enemy fire and heard of the tail gunner getting trapped in the turret and being unable to bail out. This wasn't going to happen to me. Some of the B-24's actually had these doors removed to avoid this possibility. I plugged in to the interphone and adjusted the setting on my oxygen. I also plugged in my electrically heated flying suit.

Soon the pilot gave the command to test fire our guns. I had already turned on the power to the turret and turned on the gunsight. I charged both guns and fired a short burst. The other gunners did the same. The plane vibrated as Nauman and Miller fired off short bursts at the waist guns. I could also hear Argie firing his guns in the ball turret and felt the plane shake. Hosier and Manfrida were doing the same up front. After this ritual, I settled down to scanning side to side for enemy fighters, rotating the turret and moving the guns up and down. There were very few of our own planes in formation behind us. Most were in front of us.

I began to feel airsick. I was bouncing around a lot in the turret and there was a lot of air turbulence. This, coupled with the fact that I was riding backwards, made me ill. Fortunately, I remembered to bring along an extra flak helmet. I took off my oxygen mask and puked into the helmet. I'd hoped this wouldn't happen in combat. So much for my hopes. I quickly set the helmet outside the turret and put my oxygen mask back on. At least I didn't have to worry about spilling the contents of the helmet on the floor of the plane. At this altitude it froze immediately. This airsickness would continue to plague me throughout the war and it was especially bad when I was in the turret, sitting backwards.

I looked back over my shoulder and saw Miller and Nauman manning the waist guns, intently scanning the sky. I could see the top of the ball turret rotating and knew that Argie was also scanning. We were a good crew. With this crew and a good deal of luck, I might just survive this war. It was too early to tell though, this being my first mission. On and on the formation droned, slowly climbing to reach our assigned bombing altitude.

About every 15 minutes, one of the officers called for an oxygen check. This was actually a status check on all of us, to ensure that no one lost consciousness due to a malfunction with the oxygen system. I occasionally squeezed my oxygen mask. This broke up any ice particles in the mask caused by breath condensation and kept the air flowing.

Shortly before noon we passed the I.P. (Initial Point) and turned onto the bomb run. For the next several minutes the group was on a straight course to the target. There were no deviations and we were sitting ducks for any anti-aircraft guns in the target area. It was at this point that I put on my flak helmet. I only wore it when I thought we were going to get shot at, because it was so heavy and uncomfortable. Most of the time it sat beside me in the turret. I also pulled my goggles down over my eyes. I didn't wear the goggles most of the time. Even though they had interchangeable lenses, I could see better without them.

Before I heard "bombs away" over the intercom, I looked off to my left and, in the distance saw black puffs of smoke. This was the flak I heard so much about. It wasn't close to our formation and was no threat at all. I couldn't hear the flak bursts. They were too far away and I had my leather helmet with earphones on. I continued to see the puffs for about five minutes. The flak appeared to be a few thousand feet lower than our formation. I didn't know what the Germans were shooting at, because I could see no planes close to the flak. When the bombs were dropped the plane lifted, relieved of its payload. Shortly thereafter we turned abruptly away from the target, in a diving turn on what was known as the "rally".

After we left the target area, I saw several specks in the distance, which I believed were fighter planes. They kept their distance, flying high overhead and off to one side of the formation. I could also see P-38's in the distance, but the 38's showed no interest. As the specks drew closer I could see that they were single engine fighters, and as they got closer still, I could see they were P-51's. I felt very protected.

Our trip back to Italy was uneventful. This was an easy mission and I hoped that they would all be this easy. I was particularly grateful for the fighter support. I thought the Germans would be crazy to try to attack with all these fighters protecting us. As we flew south, descending gradually, Baker told us we could take off our oxygen masks. After we left enemy territory, I left my turret and helped Argie up out of the ball turret.

I looked out a waist window and saw the Adriatic below us. We were still flying in formation, but the formation was much looser now that we weren't over enemy territory. Miller and Argie were in better spirits than when we had taken off. I felt better too, despite my airsickness.

When we got back to base we circled and eventually landed when our turn came, after being in the air for 8 ½ hours. In a few minutes a truck arrived to take us to debriefing. The Red Cross supplied all aircrews with doughnuts and coffee after every mission. There wasn't much for us to report at debriefing. The Flight Surgeon, Captain Johnson, gave us each a shot of whiskey. I also took Baker's, since he didn't drink. I hated to see it go to waste. I saved his portion, to be enjoyed at a later date.

November 4, 1944

Dear Mother,

As I am quite tired tonight I will make this a short one, to let you know I am well. I went on my first combat mission to-day and, as usual, when one does something new, he gets pretty tired. That is the way I feel tonight. We had to get up at 3:30 this morning, so you can see it does make a pretty long day of it. But we'll get by I guess. Can't tell you where we went today, but will at a later date. I expect you have a good idea.

So far, combat hadn't been too bad. We were trying to figure out how many missions we needed to go home. The words missions and sorties were generally used interchangeably, although there was a difference. A sortie was one trip up to the target and back. For some of the longer, tougher sorties we would get credit for two missions; hence we would have more missions than sorties. (Some of the crews before us may have finished their 50 missions with only 30 sorties.) When we arrived we needed either 50 missions or 35 sorties, whichever came first, to complete our tour. Soon this was changed to 35 sorties, regardless of the number of missions. Linz was in the northern part of Austria, quite a distance from southern Italy, but I don't recall whether it counted as one or two missions.

Baker and Scheib flew a mission without the rest of us on the 5th. It was the 100th mission for the 485th. They bombed the Florisdorf Oil Refinery at Vienna. Scheib later told us the weather was miserable while they were forming up. They entered the clouds with two other planes as they climbed to join the group. When they came out of the clouds the other two planes weren't there. They had collided in mid-air. One of the planes made it back to base and the other crashed. Two of the crew parachuted safely; the other eight men didn't make it.[2]

November 6, 1944

Dear Mother,

I just got through sweating out mail call now. It was a very long mail call.....plenty of mail... .but none for our crew. I stayed from A to Z and it was sure a long time and then the answer came "no letter today". Well, that's life I guess.

Argie and Nauman flew today with other crews so Argie is up two missions on me and Nauman is up four missions on me. I expect you have received the letter where I told you I flew my first combat mission. Well I did and we bombed Linz, Austria.

Me, Miller and Manfrida built a writing table today and also banked up our tent. I am writing this by candle light by our gas stove. I was through Naples when I got here. Have only been in one other town since. Let me know if there is very much cut from my letters. I have to get up real early in the morning, so will sign off.

I never volunteered to fly with other crews. Some of the others did, but I felt the best chance for survival was to fly with those I'd trained with and trusted most. I was particularly concerned about flying with other pilots. I had complete faith in our pilots, but didn't feel comfortable flying with other pilots that I didn't know. This belief intensified as I continued flying combat. Argie and Nauman had been assigned to fly with another crew on November 6th. They went to Vienna with Gillette's crew. They bombed by PFF (radar) since the target area was completely covered by clouds. I don't know if they hit the target, but the clouds spared them most of the murderous flak that was expected in the Vienna area.

I checked the bulletin board and saw that we were scheduled to fly again on the 7th. We got our wake up call and went through the same ritual that would become so familiar. At briefing we found out that we were going to bomb the Adige/Ora railroad bridge in northern Italy. We expected this to be a pretty easy target, since it would be a short mission and we wouldn't be over enemy territory for very long. We took off shortly after 9:00AM with 27 other bombers from our group. We were flying a B-24 J, "Blue G".

There was no scheduled fighter escort. All four bomb groups in the 55th Wing were bombing the same target, a single bridge. We were second in line, behind the 460th, and were scheduled to bomb from 17,000 feet, a pretty low altitude. Due to cloud cover we bombed from 16,000 feet. The low bombing altitude and a strong head wind worked against us. The flak was very heavy over the target. The heavy flak lasted for about four minutes and we were hit intermittently for about 30 minutes, until we got back to the Adriatic coast.

The lead ship was hit immediately after dropping its bombs and gave up the lead. We were also hit about the same time we dropped our bombs. Our plane was being bounced around from the nearby explosions. A shell fragment came through the upper turret and bounced off Hosier's flak helmet. We later found seven good-sized holes in the bomber. We didn't bother to look for small holes.

We were in better shape than many from our group. Nothing vital was hit on our plane and we made it back to base without incident. Some of the others weren't so fortunate. Of the 27 bombers that made it to the target in our group, eight received major flak damage, but made it back to friendly fields, including the mission leader. We and fourteen others received minor and semi-major damage. The few remaining bombers received no damage. A total of six crewmembers on the various bombers were injured. I have no idea how much damage the other groups had, but I would imagine they were hit just as hard as we were. I saw a lot of flak being thrown up at the groups behind us and there were several smoking B-24's as they rallied off the target.

We didn't hit the bridge, but may have damaged the approach and first span. There were at least 100 planes bombing the same bridge, but we missed the target. We were pretty shaken up when we returned. There were quite a few smoking and damaged bombers, some with feathered props, and our returning group was a lot smaller than when we started that morning. Fortunately, the missing bombers landed at fields that were closer to the front lines than ours. Planes with injured fliers on board often landed at fields farther north or at larger bases with better hospital facilities.

Nauman and I talked a lot about the flak. Nauman, as a waist gunner, could move around more than I could. As time went on, we discussed the safest places to be on the plane. Nauman thought at first that being close to the bomb bay was a good place, especially for an easy exit if we had to bail out. After seeing a plane get a direct hit in the bomb bay, and seeing the bombs explode, Nauman didn't think that was the best place to be. He talked about sitting on an ammo box, but decided against it, fearing the ammo in the box could explode. I think he finally decided to put a couple of flak vests beneath him and sit on them. As time went on, we both decided there were no safe places on a plane when people were shooting at you. On a couple of later missions, when our plane was badly damaged, Nauman opened the rear escape hatch for us so we could bail out quickly if we had to.

Long after the war ended, I talked to some of the crew members and learned that several of us took along extra flak vests and put them in strategic places for protection. It's no wonder that we seemed to use up every inch of the runway. We must have really been overloaded.

We weren't scheduled for a mission the next day, so we kept ourselves busy around the tent. The day after that we had gunnery practice. We flew over the Bay of Taranto and shot at targets on the ground. We had a lot of ammo to shoot and Suttkus came back to the waist to fire some rounds with us. All of the gunners took turns shooting from various turrets and positions. Suttkus liked to practice with us. When we flew over the coast one of our guys shot into a field, scattering a herd of sheep. He sure made them scatter and I could see the farmer on the ground, shaking his fist at us. Between the engine noise from our low-flying plane and the noise from the machine gun, it would take that farmer a while to round up his flock.

On November 11th, we were scheduled for another mission. We lost #1 engine before getting very far, so we came back. As it turned out, the mission was scrubbed anyway and the entire group returned. The weather was pretty miserable. Our pilots would never turn back from a mission unless it was absolutely necessary. As much as we all grew to hate combat, we wanted to finish our missions and go home. I believe that most of the crews felt this way. There may have been an occasional exception to this, but it was rare. The mechanical problems we experienced on our aircraft weren't due to poor maintenance, but mostly due to old, worn-out equipment. Our ground crews did everything they could to repair and maintain the bombers.

November 11, 1944

Dear Mother,

For the past two days I have had to get up before three in the morning and it sure is cold then. Then I have to fly. It sure is cold up there in the air. It would have been 55 degrees below zero at the altitude we were to fly yesterday. So, if you folks get a little cold, think of me up there at 55 degrees below or more and you will probably feel much warmer. My hands get colder than any part of my body, but I guess we will make out ok.

Oh yeah, I was going to tell you about our pilot. Boy, he sure is a swell pilot. He can really fly that plane. Everyone thinks he's ok. He is a lot better now than he was and he always was good. We came back with only three engines running yesterday. Of course, it was a practice mission and isn't credited to our combat missions. My pilot and navigator were just over here talking to us in our tent. He (the pilot) censors our mail, so you will probably notice his name on them. Some Suttkus does (censor letters). We sure have a swell navigator. Yesterday we were in some really thick clouds and he told us what we would see when we came out of them, and we did. He really knows his stuff.

When we weren't flying or training, we continued our tent improvements. I also spent time writing letters.

November 13, 1944

Dear Mother,

I went to town the other day to get a few things which we needed for our tent. We got a broom, which in the states one could buy for 29 cents and paid 80 lira or 80 cents for it. Bought a kerosene lamp made of tin and paid 500 lire or $5.00 for it. The six of us chipped in, so it didn't cost any of us much and I am sure we will get use out of it, as it is much better than candles, especially when the supply runs out of candles.

Whenever we needed to buy anything we tried to have Manfrida with us. He was Italian and he could understand the language somewhat. I don't recall that he spoke it very well, but he could understand the Italians and got us better deals than we could have on our own.

In my letters home we couldn't tell our families exactly where we were. I'd try to give little hints, expecting that my family might be able to read between the lines. My mother always wanted me to see as much as I could of the countryside and of the historic things. I don't think she ever understood that we couldn't concern ourselves with tourism. Often, what we saw, we bombed.

November 14, 1944

Dear Mother,

No, I cannot tell you just where I am, but as I have said, I am in southern Italy. I am sorry I couldn't write you more, but when I was on the boat I couldn't mail them anyway, although I did write quite a few letters, which you should have received all at once. I don't know if I told you or not, but I was aboard ship 26 long days. But I can say I didn't get seasick. It never bothered me at all. The sailors seemed to think it was rather rough at times, but it wasn't half as rough as in the air sometimes.

We are doing fine, but the weather isn't a bit in our favor now. From what I hear we have to put in 35 sorties, where in the past they put in 50 missions, but most of the sorties were double missions, and they really only had to put in 25 or 26 sorties and would have 50 missions. Now every sortie is one completed flight and we have to put in 35 of them or more. I have in 2 sorties or 3 missions, as one sortie counted as 2 missions. I don't know if this is official or not. Anyway, it will be a long time at the rate we're going before we get ours completed. Oh yeah, I went to church Sunday evening. Had a nice service.

It was frustrating that the weather was so bad. We began to feel like we'd be in Italy forever. I think I was also frustrated about the last mission. We were getting shot up and, except for the bombardier dropping his bombs, we couldn't fight back. I never lost this frustration, and it would intensify. A lot of the guys felt the same way. We'd often see our friends getting shot down or get hit ourselves, and there was nothing we could do about it, except take it.

11. Wayne with canine neighbors (November 1944)

We managed to get most of the holes in the tent plugged. We continued making improvements to our abode, which included a locking door and other amenities.

November 15, 1944

Dear Beulah (sister),

Every time I hear something about Freddy Morton or any of those old dance bands I wish I was back there again. But maybe this darn war will end someday....anyway we all hope it's not too long.

I haven't had a chance to shoot at any fighters so far and in one way I hope I don't have the opportunity and in another way I am anxious to have the honor of blowing one to bits. I am so darn angry at everything, in general. Guess I will have a quart of vino wine and sit down and celebrate my birthday, that is, if I am not on a mission. Then, as you know, I will be just sweating out my birthday, not celebrating it.

I was over to the officers' tent last night, visiting them, but the pilot and bombardier were gone to the show. The navigator explained a few formalities in navigation. It was very interesting. So Frankie (President Roosevelt) has made a lot of speeches lately. Well, I am sorta glad that I'm not hearing all that is said, as I am sure I would get tired of listening to him, especially now.

Word got around base that a crew went MIA (Missing in Action) on the 15th. There were few details, but a B-24 from the 828th Squadron didn't make it back from another mission to Linz, Austria.[3]

On November 16th, I saw that our crew was scheduled for a mission the next day.

NOTES AND REFERENCES

1 While it may have true that a couple of men aboard had completed their missions, men from the 485th were being flown to Naples on leave, including several ground personnel. Those killed were Alfred Reiss, pilot; William BeGole, copilot; Frederic Gordon, navigator; Robert Connor, flight engineer; Alex Melillo, radio operator; Billy Sears, bombardier; James Wheeler, navigator; Lloyd Arnold, crew chief; Donald Brown, ball gunner; Keith LaFrance, unknown assignment, and Leonard Lee, intelligence non-com.

2 The planes that collided were both from the 831st Squadron. One plane landed safely, but Captain Eddie Neitzel's plane went down. Two parachuted safely. Killed were Eddie Neitzel, pilot; Robert Schoener, copilot; Robert Bishop, top turret; Frank Griffin, tail gunner; Philmore Gross, radio operator; James Leturno, flight engineer; Emil Manweiler, gunner and Max Sunshine, PFF navigator.

3 This was Charles Fabry's crew and this was a secret, single-plane, bad weather raid to Linz, Austria. Fabry was killed and several others managed to evade capture when the plane went down in Yugoslavia.

Blechhammer!

On the morning of November 17th, we were awakened in the early morning hours to go through our ritual of preparing for a mission. When the curtain was pulled back from the map at briefing, there were sighs and groans from the men in the room. The ribbon on the map ended at Blechhammer, Germany, a target way up near the Polish border.[1] Our target was the Blechhammer South oil refinery. It looked like a long flight over enemy territory. Our group had already lost several planes at this target. The first commanding officer of the group, Colonel Arnold, was shot down over Blechhammer in August.

Twenty one planes took off for the mission. After assembling with other groups, we headed north. The trip up there was pretty uneventful, but it was very cold. We were joined by our P-38 escort as we continued our long journey. Two of our B-24's turned back before reaching the target. The weather was rough and I got bounced around a lot in the tail and used my extra flak helmet more often than usual.

Quite a while before we reached the target we discovered we were low on oxygen. Since we were above 20,000 feet, oxygen was a must for survival. Baker made the decision to continue on to the target. McLawhorn came around with portable oxygen bottles, replenishing our supply. When we approached the target there was flak in the distance, but we didn't get hit. The target was cloud-covered, but we dropped our bombs anyway.

Shortly after "bombs away", our bomber went into a steep dive. This was not a good sign. I slid back out of my turret, thinking we were going down. After several thousand feet, we leveled out. Shortly thereafter, I learned what happened. Over the target area Baker ran out of oxygen and slumped over the controls. Scheib, still conscious, put the plane into a dive in order to get to a lower altitude where the crew could breathe normally. Both Suttkus and McLawhorn had also passed out in the front of the plane.

After Scheib got to a lower altitude and leveled out, the three other officers regained consciousness. I saw that we were alone now. As we dived, the formation passed above us, leaving us behind them. This was not a good feeling, with hundreds of miles to travel over enemy territory. Before too long a P-38 descended from altitude to join us, off our left wing. Scheib later told me that Nauman tapped him on the shoulder and pointed out the window at the P-38. A few minutes later Scheib looked out the right cockpit window and saw a lone P-51 off our right wing. The plane was very close and had a red tail on it. Scheib could see the pilot clearly as the pilot unsnapped his oxygen mask, looking over at Jim. With the oxygen mask away from the pilot's face, Scheib could see that the pilot was black. He realized our P-51 escort was from the 332nd Fighter Group, which much later became known as the Tuskegee Airmen.[2]

It was comforting to have our escort. Even at the lower altitude I felt like I would freeze to death. Our escorts, low on fuel, left before we reached the Adriatic coast. We too, were low on fuel. Baker decided to head for Vis, concerned that we didn't have enough fuel to make it home. Ditching or bailing out over the Adriatic was something that none of us wanted. B-24's had a structural weakness and a tendency to break in half when ditching in the water. Many airmen drowned after bailing out over the Adriatic, some trapped in their parachute lines. Either possibility was not very comforting.

Vis is a tiny island about 40 miles off the coast of Yugoslavia, in the Adriatic. It was a haven for 15th Air Force planes and crews that couldn't make it back to Italy. Vis was only about three miles long and the actual runway was about 3500 feet long. It was an amphibious operating base for Yugoslav Partisans, British Commandos and American Rangers. The British also kept a few Spitfires there for attacks on the Yugoslav mainland. The runway was gravel and was situated in a mountain valley on the island. It was not an ideal setting, but it was certainly a lifesaver for many 485th Bomb Group crews who couldn't make it back to Venosa, due to battle damage or low on fuel.

As we approached Vis, another assessment was made by the pilots and Nauman, and they thought we had enough fuel to make it home. We did, and landed at Venosa, with less than 50 gallons in each fuel tank. After returning, I learned that two of our group's bombers did land at Vis and that one plane went down over Yugoslavia after running out of fuel.[3]

The next day we hung around the tent. I was exhausted and didn't do much at all. I still felt frozen.

November 19, 1944

Dear Mother,

We six of our crew played a little football this morning. Had quite a lot of fun and it was good exercise for us. Well, I haven't flown since day before yesterday. It was a very long mission and it sure was cold. I don't believe I was ever so cold in my whole life as I was then and I don't wish to be that cold again. My fingers on one of my hands are still a little numb. In case you want to know where we went, well it

was a target up at Blechhammer, Germany. You may be able to find it on the map as it is quite large I think.

On November 19th, I looked at the roster and saw we were scheduled for a mission on the 20th. It wasn't the best way to spend my birthday and I had hoped to have the day free. It was not to be. At briefing we learned that our target again was the Blechhammer South Oil Refinery. We must have missed the target last time. This time I think I groaned.

I hoped that we'd get a plane with a good oxygen system this time and one that wasn't so hard on gas. Our pilots were both extremely good at conserving gas and Nauman was excellent at transferring fuel to maximize our mileage. What we hoped for was a good plane. Nauman and Argie were grounded due to sickness, so without our engineer and assistant engineer, we'd be flying with replacements.

Take off was uneventful. There were 27 planes that joined up with the 460th Bomb Group. We eventually joined up with the other two groups in our bomb wing, with our group being third in line. Our P-38 escort joined us. The weather was much clearer than last time and it wasn't so cold. As we approached the target area, we ran into heavy flak. This time it was accurate and very close to us. I could hear the explosions and see the red centers of the flak bursts. They were bursting all over the place. The tail turret was bouncing up and down. I could smell the cordite from the German shells, even through the oxygen mask. It smelled like rotten eggs.

Several planes were smoking. I saw a plane from one of the other groups take a direct hit, break apart and go down. I saw no parachutes. I was trying to make myself as small as possible. My steel helmet was pulled down over most of my face. I couldn't see much, but I didn't have to worry about German fighters attacking us in all this flak. I had a flak vest under my seat and my legs were pulled up and tight against my body. This was not the way I intended to spend my birthday!

12. 465th BG B-24 explodes over Blechhammer on November 20, 1944
(15th AF photo)

After we dropped our bombs and started our rally off the target, I saw one of our group falling behind. From its markings I could see it was from our squadron, Blue H. One of its engines was feathered and it continued to fall farther and farther behind, all alone, until it was out of sight. I had a sick feeling and realized it didn't have much chance of making it home. I later learned it went down.[4]

We were in heavy flak a total of about six minutes. Later we counted six holes in our plane, but for now we just concentrated on making it home. Many of our planes were damaged. After we were over the Adriatic, several of the more seriously damaged planes left formation, looking for closer fields. We made it back to base without incident. The flak hit nothing vital on our plane. Four in our group received major damage and twelve, like us, had minor damage. Several of the planes that left formation over the Adriatic landed at friendly fields, to return to Venosa later.

The hits on the target this time were excellent, so that made me feel a little better, but what a way to spend my birthday. The mission lasted 9½ hours and we were all exhausted when we landed.

November 21, 1944

Dear Mother,

Well, as you know, yesterday was my 22nd birthday and I can assure you I will never forget it either. I can't say I enjoyed it, but you can guess why. I don't believe it would be very hard to understand if you knew where I was. But everything went ok. I just hope that next year I can spend my birthday with all of you folks.

NOTES AND REFERENCES

1 Blechhammer is now in Poland, near Kedzierzyn-Kozle.

2 Repeated efforts to identify the fighter pilots have been unsuccessful.

3 The plane that went down over Yugoslavia was an 829th B.S. plane, piloted by Charles Stewart. The entire crew eventually made it safely back to Italy, with most of them returning in January.

4 This crew was Lt. Jerome Warner's crew, a new crew that had recently arrived at Venosa. The plane went down in Czechoslovakia and the entire crew bailed out, was captured and became POWs. This information was confirmed in a 2005 phone interview with Frank Hennessey, one of the gunners, who landed in the midst of an SS encampment.

The Air War Continues

We were scheduled for another mission to Germany on the 22nd of November. We got up early and went through the normal routine, only to have to cancel the mission when one of the superchargers went out before take-off. One B-24 crashed a few minutes after take-off. Three of the crew were able to bail out, but the others died in the crash.[1] Due to bad weather the group bombed the alternate target, Salzburg, Austria. Several of the aircraft were hit by flak and six men from various crews were wounded by the flak.

Since we couldn't fly we hung around our tent, sewing up holes and making other repairs. Our first holiday overseas, Thanksgiving, was coming up and we tried not to think about it. Miller had a little radio and he spent much of the day trying to get it to work. A few of us went out to the Enlisted Men's Club that night and drank too much. We suffered the next day. My mother belonged to WCTU, which stood for Women's Christian Temperance Union. She was opposed to drinking any sort of alcohol and was always mentioning in her letters that she hoped I wasn't drinking. I saw no point in having her worry.

November 23, 1944

Dear Mother,

Well, today is Thanksgiving Day for us. I see we will have turkey, but don't know yet how it will taste. I hope it is pretty good. It is in the morning now and I hear that we are going to have to work on the line today, but that is better than going on a mission. I expect you don't know it, but I was at one camp when I just landed in Italy, was there several days, then moved to another, then I came to this place. So this is my third place in Italy. Yes, I am seeing all I can, although right around here there isn't much one can see.

No, I am not drinking, only a bottle of beer or a glass of wine once in awhile, but not to a great extent. You mentioned about having my prayer book. Yes, I have it and I read it quite often. After one is once in combat he gets religious in a hurry. I go to church quite often and am going to keep it up. The last few missions I have prayed to myself before going on the bomb run as one sure needs to, I'm convinced now. Don't worry about me as I am making it ok and I hope to continue to.

Oh, last night Miller got his little radio working. It isn't very loud, but could get a few Italian stations... sounded good anyway. I am about 150 miles from that city you mentioned. Will finish this letter this evening after we have our turkey to let you know how it was. I am not expecting it to be too good as the army doesn't prepare food very well, usually.

Well, we had a lovely Thanksgiving dinner for overseas today. One can thank God we got to eat turkey and not K rations, which many boys had to eat today, most likely. I just heard there is going to be a stage show at eight o'clock tonight, so may go to it. If you can find a harmonica please get me one and send it to me.

We flew no more missions throughout the remainder of November. Missions were scheduled, then canceled. The weather was just too miserable. It was rainy and foggy much of the time. A few planes from the group flew one other mission in November, a night mission on the 25th. We didn't hear much about the night missions. Usually only three or four bombers went on these missions and took off several minutes apart. We assumed that they were night bombing missions, using radar to bomb, but we never heard the specific details.[2] During the day some of us worked on the flight line. At least it kept us busy and kept our minds off combat.

Miller, Hosier, Manfrida and I decided to go to Bari, which was on the east coast of Italy, not too far from our base. We were able to hitch a ride with some engineers in a 10-wheeler truck. Bari was where 15th Air Force headquarters was located and seemed more civilized than the other towns I'd seen and was less affected by the war. It was certainly much cleaner than Naples. We spent the day sightseeing around Bari and came back with the engineers. It was a long day, since the truck broke down on the way back, but it was something different, a change of pace. We got back to the base about 3:30AM. I was able to buy a guitar in a little shop. I had a nice guitar at home that I really enjoyed playing, and playing my new guitar would keep my mind occupied and give me something to do in the tent.

November 27, 1944

Dear Mother,

Yesterday, Miller, Hosier, Manfrida and I went to Bari. It wasn't our first intention, but as we found a ride we decided we'd go sightseeing. Well, I have to admit that so far it is the most civilized place I have been over here. We had a lot of fun, although we nearly froze on our way back to camp. It wasn't so cold, but we were just plain stupid and didn't take our overcoats with us.

I expect you will think I am crazy for this, but I bought me a guitar. It was for $25 but I got the guy down to $17 and so I got it. I figure I can get that much out of it while overseas and *have something to do in my spare time. My fingers are sore from playing it all the way or nearly (all the way) from there last night. The other boys sang. We had quite a time.*

It sure makes one's morale go down when one doesn't get mail often. I go to another mail call and the same answer, "no letter today". What a life, but I say to myself I guess I can live through it. Many have already.

November 28, 1944

Dear Mother,

It was really foggy this morning and tonight it rained and still is raining, I guess, although at this minute three guys are trying to sing "Oh Susanna" and I couldn't hear rain-drops on the tent to save my neck. Oh, say Mother, if you can find any 127 or 616 films please send me whatever you can get. I know they are hard to find, but I would like to get some pictures over here. Miller has a 616 camera and Suttkus, the navigator, has a 127 camera I can borrow. I thought maybe the girls could try and get them if they are downtown some-time.

December 1, 1944

Dear Mother,

We are having some awful weather here now. It is always foggy in the morning and it has been raining for several days. It sure is sloppy around here and we haven't any over-shoes yet. The officers are going to try and buy some in their PX in town for us, as we all have wet feet tonight.

Finally, on the 5th of December, we were scheduled for a mission the next day. At briefing we learned the target was a marshaling yard at Hegyeshalom, Hungary. It turned out to be a "milk run". I don't think we took any flak hits at all. There was a little flak when we passed over Gyor, Hungary. A couple of planes received minor flak hits, but we all made it back safely. Miller thought we got some good hits on the target. It was a

13. In a lighter moment 828th B.S. cooks protect themselves from irate diners. (Tony Siller is front left in photo.)

relatively short mission of seven hours and forty minutes, so we weren't too tired when we got back. There was a USO show that night that we attended, featuring two women singing and playing various kinds of music. They weren't famous or well-known, but it was nice to see anyone and anything from back in the States.

Between missions the work continued on our tent. There was always some improvement to be made. If I wasn't working on the tent I was working on the flight line during the day. I played my new guitar whenever I got the chance, usually in the evening.

December 9, 1944

Dear Mother,

I haven't gotten any mail from you folks, but will write anyhow. Well, I completed my fifth mission several days ago. If they are all like that one I couldn't kick, but that is probably one in a hundred. Last night Suttkus, our navigator, came over and Hosier and he played cards against Manfrida and

Argie. Guess I will go up and have the Italian barber shave me. They only charge 5 cents for a shave and 10 cents for a haircut, so it really doesn't pay to shave myself. I just got through evening chow. We had chicken tonight, but it really didn't taste much like chicken.

I know you folks like to give me advice and I appreciate it. That's one thing parents are for is to start the young folks on the right track, but the young folks usually don't appreciate it. I am thinking a little bit of getting a little education after this is over, but nothing where I am attached to this darn army...am disgusted with it and how it is run. I don't want to be away from old friends for years like I have since Pearl Harbor, as that isn't good either.

On the 10th, we were scheduled to bomb a target at Brux, Czechoslovakia. The weather was absolutely horrible enroute to the target. The mission was canceled but our field was completely closed in. Of the 29 bombers that took off, only two managed to find our home field. After several hours Baker was ordered by the group commander to scout the weather toward our base. We left formation and headed back to Venosa. The clouds and fog were thick, even at ground level. To make matters worse, the radio went out. I wondered how we'd ever make it back. Since we were not over enemy territory, I wasn't in my turret. I took up a position over the camera hatch with my parachute on, ready to make a quick exit. Baker and Scheib finally found a break in the clouds and we were able to land at Pantanella, a base not far from ours.[3] We took a truck back to Venosa. We were exhausted by the time we got home. The rest of the group landed at bases all around the area. All managed to get back safely. It had been a very long, tense day, and our pilots had once again gotten us home safely.

December 11, 1944

Dear Mother,

I can't write decent today. Yesterday I guess that flying ruined my brain. Anyway, that's the way I feel today. We were

14. Baker's crew in the mud. Front (L-R): Scheib, Suttkus, Nauman, Whiting. Back (L-R): Argie, Miller, Manfrida, McLawhorn, Baker.

on a practice formation flight and it became so cloudy after we got in the air that we couldn't find the field or any field, so we had to stay above the clouds for five hours waiting for the clouds to go away, so we could find the field and land. Well, it did and we landed, but it wasn't our field, and a truck from our field had to come and get us. So you can see what an awful time we had. We got up at 4:30 in the morning and didn't get back to our tent 'til 8:30 (at night), so you can see we had quite a long day of it.

I went into Venosa with some of the guys on the 12th. It gave us something to do and got us out of our soggy, wet tent. Venosa was just a small town and there wasn't much to see. Anything was better than sitting around in the tent, with that lingering odor of wet canvas. We were scheduled for a mission on the 13th, but it was scrubbed at briefing. Weather was making it impossible to fly. None of us relished the thought of going into combat again, but we wanted to get it over so we could go home.

15. Sgt. Lester York (center) with *The Character.*

December 13, 1944

Dear Mother,

Yes, that is sorta mixed up about the missions and sorties but it is straightened out OK now. When we started we had to put in 35 sorties. Of course a sortie is (one trip) to the target and back to base. I have 5 in so that leaves 30 to go yet. It rained again last night and this morning, so you can see how much it rains here. I sure wish we had overshoes to wear. We are in mud up to our knees, practically.

Miller, Argie, Hosier, and I went to town yesterday. There wasn't much going on, but we had a little fun and also got away from camp for several hours. We were in a place where a guy was playing an accordion and there wasn't anyone playing the guitar, so I played with him for awhile.....had quite a time. Of course, he was Italian and I couldn't play too many Italian songs. Boy, it sure brightens up one's morale to get mail.

On the 14th, we checked the board and saw we were scheduled for a mission the next day. On the morning of the 15th, we were awakened for the mission, attended the briefing, and learned that our target was a marshaling yard at Salzburg, Austria. The ship assigned to us was Blue M, *The Character. The Character* was one of the original bombers assigned to the group and had a lot of missions to her credit. We'd flown this bomber on an earlier mission.

The crew chief, Sgt. Lester York, was a religious man and he always got the crew together before a mission to pray for a safe return. It was rumored that Sgt. York was a distant relative of Sgt. Alvin York of WWI fame, a Congressional Medal of Honor recipient. I don't know if there was any validity to that rumor, but it was comforting to have Sgt. York praying for us. We could certainly use all the help we could get.

As it turned out, we had mechanical trouble on this mission. The nose wheel wouldn't stay up and we had to turn around and come back. We spent the remainder of the day helping out on the flight line, cleaning guns on bombers and doing whatever we could to assist the ground crews. Since I had been to armament school, I also helped repair turrets that weren't functioning properly. In the evening, we checked the board and saw we were scheduled for another mission the next day.

The target for the 16th turned out to be Brux, Czechoslovakia. It was a long way up there. At the time, I actually thought Brux was in Germany. We took off and formed up behind the 460th Bomb Group. We intended to bomb by radar due to the poor weather conditions. Our deputy lead aircraft turned back with mechanical problems and the lead ship's radar wasn't functioning properly. The lead plane decided to follow the 460th and bomb with them. We were on the final run when the 460th turned off the bomb run, the target being a synthetic oil refinery. Our group had no choice but to follow. We followed the 460th and bombed oil installations at Pilsen, Czechoslovakia. We were in flak over Pilsen for about four minutes total, but took no major hits.

Bomb photos showed that we missed the target by about five miles. This precision bombing wasn't all it was cracked up to be. I never thought much about what we may have hit, but I hoped we'd just plowed up empty fields. It was dark by the time we reached the Italian coast. We made three passes at the airfield in the dark before we were able to get the plane down safely. All the crews were exhausted and there wasn't much partying that night.

December 17, 1944

Dear Mother,

We went on a mission yesterday and I wouldn't be surprised if you have heard about this as it was quite an effort. Our target was Brux. No, I am not suffering from the cold. We make out OK. Don't worry about me as a GI always makes a go of it, somehow. It really doesn't get too cold in degrees here, but it is forever raining.

I went down and cleaned the guns on my turret today, so they really ought to shoot good now. I hear there is a guy in the next tent over from ours from Flandreau, South Dakota. Haven't talked to him yet, but I am going to (talk to him) one of these days.

We were scheduled for another mission on the 18th. At briefing we found out the target was again Blechhammer. I'd hoped that this synthetic oil refinery had been destroyed by now. That wasn't the case. Some of our group had also bombed Blechhammer on the 17th, without any losses. It would be another long, cold mission for us.

After we'd formed up with the other groups, it was very comforting to see that we had lots of fighters protecting us. There were 60-80 P-38's and P-51's that stayed with us all through enemy territory. They weren't necessarily close to our group all the time, but they were there. The weather conditions over the target were miserable. The target was completely cloud-covered, so bombing was done by radar. Several crews thought the bombs landed south of the refinery. We received no flak damage, although there was some flak over the target. One of the bombers from the 828th Squadron was shot down by flak near Zagreb, Yugoslavia. This bomber was one of three that had been unable to keep up with the formation.[4]

While returning from the mission, one of the bombers from our squadron left the formation. We found out that it ditched in the Adriatic and several of the crew drowned, including the pilot. Baker knew the copilot on the crew, Harley Beard, and Harley survived the ditching. Baker tells the story best. "....we flew over the Adriatic to avoid flak batteries. As we approached the Italian coast, the pilot of the lead plane radioed us to ask if we would lead the squadron back to base, since they had not dropped their bombs on target or jettisoned them in the Adriatic. We led the squadron back to base safely.

Beard's plane flew back over the sea and ran out of fuel. The crew bailed out and most of them were lost. Later, Harley came to our tent and told us about parachuting into the sea. He was saved by pulling the emergency cord on his Mae West (life vest). This brought him to the surface. He said it felt as though he had gone down about 1000 feet and didn't expect to come to the surface before he drowned."[5]

After returning from the mission, we went back to our tents for a while and then went to chow. After our usual meal, we checked the mission board and saw our crew's name on the list. It was unusual to go on missions two days in a row, so I figured the mission would be a short milk run. This was not to be, as the briefing revealed our target was once again Blechhammer. The target was again completely obscured and a decision was reached to bomb an alternate target. Miller thought we bombed Graz, Austria, but the official records indicated that we bombed Maribor,

Yugoslavia. We didn't take any flak hits and it was a relatively short mission, since we picked up a strong tail wind on the way home.

December 20, 1944

Dear Mother,

It was my turn to stand mail call tonight and I just got back a few minutes ago. There wasn't any first class mail at all tonight. I expected several letters tonight as it has been several days since I have gotten any mail.

You asked what I have been doing. They sorta had us going for several days up 'til today. We flew three missions in four days. All of them were well up in Germany. One was not too far from Berlin and the others were more over to the east of there. They were all long missions. Well, I have got in eight now, so that is 27 left to go. Every one means closer to the end, although I am still a long way from there. But it is beginning to look a little more encouraging all the time as we knock them off.

Our ball gunner was grounded for the past two, so he has six in, instead of eight. I went on sick call the same night as I had a bad cold also, but he told the Captain how he felt and he (Captain Johnson) grounded him. But I, as always, just told him I had a little cold and asked him for an inhaler, and so he didn't ground me. I am glad he didn't as I want to put in my missions with the whole crew, instead of with another crew.

The weather here isn't good at all for flying. I was a little scared yesterday and I wasn't the only one. We were flying in so thick of clouds we couldn't see the other planes next to us and I was afraid we were going to run into another one, so I had my chute on and was ready to jump. But everything was OK.

Several nights ago a U.S.O. camp show was here. It sure was good. Several girls from the states, and also some men. It was very good, all of it. This afternoon the American Red Cross had a bunch here; it was a vaudeville act and we all enjoyed it. They had a small band and it sure was snappy. There were also four men who used to perform in Ringling Brothers and Barnum and Bailey Circus and they did some swell acts. It sure makes one feel good to have entertainment like that. We have a swell Special Services Officer here and I think he does a lot to get us entertainment.

Some of the boys put an extension onto our tent today, so we'll have more room. Oh, I don't know if I told you, but lately we have been having quite a few fresh eggs and, boy, do they taste good compared with those powdered eggs. Come to think of it, eggs are $.40 apiece here.

We can get five to seven dollars a carton for cigarettes, selling them to the Italians but, as you know, we aren't supposed to sell them. Anyway, we don't. That is some profit, buy them for $.05 a package and sell them for $.50 to $.70 a package. But that is black market and there is plenty of that overseas, as well as in the states. The way I look at it is, why sell them to the Italians, when they are over here for us boys, and the people in the states are sacrificing to have them sent over here for the boys. I think the girls in the states need them, as I hear they have started smoking pipes now.

Our tent, although not a thing of beauty, was becoming fairly comfortable. We now had two side extensions, an enclosed entryway and a nearly-completed tufa block floor. We even installed a few windows, although there wasn't much to see when looking out, except lots of other tents. The windows did allow light to enter in the day time, making it less cave-like. Christmas was approaching. The weather didn't help our spirits any, but we tried to keep busy so we wouldn't be too homesick.

We didn't have any missions scheduled for a few days. On Christmas Eve most of us went to church. Some of the guys in nearby tents celebrated by getting drunk and setting off flares. Fortunately, there were no casualties. On Christmas Day we slept in.

December 25, 1944

Dear Mother,

Here it is, Christmas. I had my dinner about an hour and a half ago. It was a pretty fine meal, but I can't say I enjoyed it as much as I did the Thanksgiving meal. Today was a dreary day. We enlisted men in our crew just sat around, talking about old times and about the farm. Nauman, Miller, and I went to church yesterday. They had a swell service and the chapel was decorated so pretty.

The officers, two of them (Baker and Suttkus) just came by and asked us if we were going to church this evening, but none of us feel like it tonight. Did I tell you that Baker made 1st lieutenant and Suttkus made 2nd lieutenant (from flight officer)? I'm sure glad to see that. I hope Baker makes captain before we go back. He is a swell pilot.

Miller just came in with the sad news that there is to be no mail call tonight, so we get to wait another day. What a life. I'm beginning to wonder what we are fighting for. But I guess a guy just gets to feeling that way in times of lonesomeness. It's still raining here. I guess it will never quit.

On Christmas night we checked the mission board and saw we were on the list again. At briefing we saw the target was again Blechhammer. There were lots of groans. The mission itself started out pretty uneventful. We fell in behind the 460th Bomb Group near Bari, Italy. Our P-38 escorts joined us as we headed north. They eventually left and we were joined by P-51's, which provided cover to Blechhammer and back to the Yugoslavian coast.

We ran into heavy flak on the bomb run. It was very intense. I wondered how we could make it through it, but we did. Miller, looking out the waist window, saw the tail get shot off "White D", a ship from the 830th Squadron. He saw no chutes, but other crews saw one parachute.[6] I did my usual routine of making myself as small as possible. Somehow we made it through without

16. The nose of *Hell's Angel*

any major hits. **(See Appendix A for recent information about this crew and plane.)**

On the way home over northern Yugoslavia, a bomber from the 831ˢᵗ Squadron ran out of gas. It was Lt. Blood's plane. I had gotten to know one of the gunners on his crew, Tom Tamraz, fairly well and spent some time with him around the base. I watched as the parachutes blossomed out of the bomber. I reported to the pilot what was happening. I continued to watch, hoping the entire crew had time to get out before the big bomber took its final plunge. I counted 11 chutes, reporting this to the pilot. Baker's comment over the intercom was "Count 'em again Whitey", and I did. I reported to Baker that there were definitely 11 chutes, and he told me to count again, saying there were only ten men on the plane. My count remained the same and I don't think Baker believed I could count.

Lt. Blood and his crew were flying *Hell's Angel* when they went down, one of the original olive drab B-24's in the group. At debriefing we confirmed that my count was correct. Captain

Johnson, our flight surgeon, was flying in *Hell's Angel* that day, and bailed out with the crew.

The loss of this crew bothered me more than some of the other losses I'd seen, because I knew some of this crew. I started out on my first mission with Lt. Blood. Even though we hadn't gotten off on the right foot, I bore him no ill will. I knew Captain Johnson because I'd gone to him for my physical when I first arrived and had also seen him for colds and at the end of missions. I knew Tamraz because we'd had a few drinks together. I had seen some of the other gunners when we worked together on the flight line. It was a good sign that all of them were able to get out of the plane safely. They were a long distance from home, in German-occupied territory, so the chances of their safe return were slim.

December 28, 1944

Dear Mother,

I caught a bad head cold and sinus infection from washing my hair. I would go on sick call but they would just do the same thing, hot compresses, and also ground me. I don't want to be grounded because, if the crew flies, I want to fly also, if I have to crawl around to do it. I will be OK, so don't worry about me. I had to work this morning down on the line. I didn't do much, just put in several hours.

I put in another mission on the 26th. We got back OK, more than I can say for some. It was again way up in Germany. I have been to one place up there 5 different times, I mean in that vicinity. I only have in 9 missions though, so I've still got 26 to go.

I'm satisfied, although if I had it over I might have done it different, but don't think I did too bad by choosing what I did. Anyway, I am thinking that people hadn't ought to talk about me not trying to do my part.

NOTES AND REFERENCES

1 This was Lt. Malcolm Dailey's 829th B.S. crew. Seven of the men were killed in the crash, which occurred about ten miles southeast of the airfield. Those killed were Malcolm Dailey, pilot; Maurice Miller, copilot; Raymond Zwinak, bombardier; Elvis Gates, flight engineer; Harry Morton, radio operator; Fred Pfaehler, gunner and Gordon Sherman, gunner.

2 These night missions, codenamed "Lonewolf" were single plane raids. They were flown only at night or in extremely bad weather and were designed to harass the civilians by keeping them in bomb shelters and out of the factories.

3 Pantanella was the home of the 464th and 465th Bomb Groups, both 55th Wing groups.

4 This was an 828th B.S. plane, piloted by Captain Joseph Gill. The entire crew made it back safely from Yugoslavia.

5 Of the 11 men on this crew, three were killed when they drowned in the Adriatic and most of the others were injured. Those killed were Robert Gillette, pilot; Harry Twichell, bombardier, and John Hirsch, top turret gunner.

6 The plane was an 830th B.S., plane flown by Lt. Lindell's 828th B.S. crew. The entire nine-man crew was killed.

7

Visiting Our "Little Friends"

We were scheduled for a mission on the 29th. It would be to the marshaling yard in Verona, Italy, and it looked like a short mission for a change. We were unable to locate the other groups after take-off, so the 485th headed for the target alone. There was flak for about five minutes as we approached the target. Most of it was inaccurate, with only a few bursts being close enough to do damage. We didn't suffer any major damage. On our return from the mission, the turbo supercharger on #2 engine went out, so the pilots feathered the engine. We were able to keep up with the formation since we were descending.

Colonel Tomhave, our commander, didn't go on this mission. On our return, the weather was so bad the Colonel hopped into a B-25 at our field, and flew out over the Adriatic to guide the formation back to base. Our squadron was still unable to follow due to the haze, and we landed at Ramitelli, a fighter base and home of the 332nd Fighter Group, the "Red Tails". There were seventeen bombers that landed at this short fighter strip and our B-24's were stacked up at the end of the runway. The black fighter pilot who had escorted us to friendly territory back in November was from this group. Everyone at this base was black.

After we landed, we were housed with some of the enlisted men from the 99th Fighter Squadron. They treated us like royalty. All of these men were well-educated and extremely professional. We could not have been treated better. They even gave up their bunks for us and slept elsewhere. There was plenty of food and it seemed better than the food we got at our base.

The weather didn't get any better the next day. The rain continued, but it was a nice break for us. A couple of the 99th guys were excellent musicians and I really enjoyed listening to them play, particularly the guitar music. On the 31st the rain continued. We ran up the engines on our plane, but there was no way we'd be taking off in this kind of weather.

A decision was reached to send most of the crew back to our base by truck. This would make the take-off weight of the plane less and make it easier and safer for the plane to take off, since their fighter runway was much shorter than ours. We headed back to our base by truck, accompanied by some of the gunners from other crews. We were back at Venosa in time to do a little New Year's Eve celebrating at the Enlisted Men's Club. It wasn't like home and there were no women, but there was alcohol. I drank my share. Nauman and Miller stayed with the plane, so we had to celebrate without them. I drank their share, too.

Our tent was in poor shape. It snowed on January 1st, making living conditions worse. There were several inches of snow on the ground. Some tents in the 831st Squadron area collapsed due to the weight of the snow. Our officers' tent had some pretty severe damage. We tried to do a few minor repairs on our tent, in order to keep it from collapsing. When the snow melted, it was a muddy mess everywhere.

January 1, 1945

Dear Mother,

We went on a mission on the 29th and on the way back to base the weather got so bad we were forced to land at another field. It was a Negro fighter field. I lived in a tent two nights with Negroes. They treated us very nice and gave us rations and we had a big time listening to their experiences. They were close to the Front in the Tunisian campaign and also in the invasion of Sicily and Italy. We came back by truck last night, some of us. We left some of the crew there to bring back the plane when weather permits. Just us gunners and the bombardier came back. That was my 10th mission. We were up to Verona, Italy, bombing on that mission.

Don't worry about me spending my money for drink as I don't care for this Italian poison water. Our crew doesn't gamble, so that is one consolation. Our bombardier does (gamble) once in a while. Last night he won $400 shooting dice.

Several of my buddies just got back from town. Tony, that Italian boy who works here on the field, wanted them and me to come in and see him today, so they went. I didn't care to go. I guess they had a good time. Anyway, they learned how people live over here.

The remainder of our crew returned on January 3rd. There was about five inches of snow on the ground and runway when they returned. Those of us who came back earlier learned that a very touching letter had been left in the cockpit of each bomber, for the pilots to find when they flew back to our base. The 332nd Fighter Group was truly a professional unit.

Our entire crew enjoyed their stay at Ramitelli. Scheib wrote to his mother on his return. Here is an excerpt from his letter to his mother:

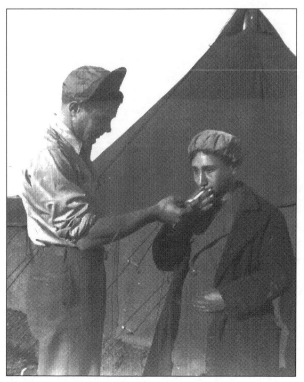

17. Tony and Manfrida

Dear Mom,

Haven't written for the past few days because I was away from "home" for nearly a week. We flew a mission to North-ern Italy and when we returned our field was closed due to weather. We landed at a P-51 fighter field and couldn't get off for 5 days. All of the pilots and ground crew were Ne-groes. They treated us like kings! I slept with a pilot from Kansas City and he couldn't do enough for me. He shared his PX rations with me and wouldn't let me get gas for his stove, water, etc.

When we were getting ready to leave I found the enclosed note on the Radio Operator's table in our ship. Those boys seem to have a high regard for the bomber pilots and I know that those Mustangs look mighty comforting on the way to and from a target!

We were forced to drop out of formation once coming back from Blechhammer due to an oxygen leak. A P-51 and a P-38 sat on either wing all the way back. Man, they are beautiful up there.

We respected all of our fighter escorts, but we'd developed a fondness for the "Red Tails". I felt safer when they were up there with us. Maybe it was my imagination, but they seemed to stay a little closer to the bombers than some of the other units.

Here is what the letter said:

TO THE VISITING PILOTS AND CREWS:[1]

YOU HAVE BEEN THE GUESTS OF THE 332ND ALL NEGRO FIGHTER GROUP. WE HOPE THAT OUR FACILITIES, SUCH AS THEY ARE, WERE SUITABLE AND ADEQUATE ENOUGH TO HAVE MADE YOUR STAY HERE A PLEASANT ONE. ON BEHALF OF COLONEL DAVIS AND THE COMMAND, I EXTEND TO YOU OUR MOST HEARTY WISHES FOR A HAPPY NEW YEAR AND MANY HAPPIER LANDINGS. YOU ARE WELCOME TO RETURN HERE AT ANY TIME AND I AM SURE THAT WE CAN MAKE YOUR STAY AN ENJOYABLE ONE. THE PILOTS OF THIS COMMAND HAVE EXPRESSED THEIR DESIRES TO HAVE IT MADE CLEAR THAT IT IS A PLEASURE TO BE ABLE TO PROTECT YOU AND LOOK AFTER YOUR WELL-BEING BOTH IN THE AIR AND HERE ON THE GROUND. REMEMBER, WHEN YOU ARE UP THERE AND SEE THE RED TAILED MUSTANGS IN THE SKY, THEY ARE YOUR FRIENDS OF THE 332ND FIGHTER GROUP. HERE IS HOPING FOR A QUICK ENDING OF THE WAR AND A BETTER AND MORE PEACEFUL WORLD.

> *MANY HAPPY LANDINGS*
> *Eugene D. Weaver*
> *Capt., Air Corps*
> *Public Relations O.*

(See Appendix B for copy of actual letter.)

NOTES AND REFERENCES

1 Jim Scheib revealed in a phone conversation in early 2001 that he saved the original letters. He said the letter meant so much to him at the time that he immediately mailed it home to his mother after his return to Venosa, so it wouldn't get lost. Other airmen in the 485th BG who were at Ramitelli described similar experiences.

A Mission in Photos

Although there was no such thing as a typical mission for the 485th Bomb Group, the planning and execution was similar (or even the same) for many of them. What follows is a series of photos, taken at Venosa and on various combat missions, on different dates throughout the group's history, depicting what occurred on a mission.

18. Mechanics preparing *Winona Belle* for next day's mission.

19. Captain Allen Meister, 828th B.S. lead bombardier and Captain Perry Updike, 828th B.S. intelligence officer, review mission plans before combat mission.

20. Unidentified 485th Officers review maps before combat mission.

21. Mechanic clears snow from 485th plane in preparation for mission.

22. Men gather in front of 828th B.S. mess hall before breakfast.

23. After breakfast, the men attend briefing (Sept 6, 1944 mission).

24. The briefing ends with a prayer by Chaplain Golder.

25. 830th B.S. crew chief Howard Megaffee rotates prop on his plane before a mission. This forced oil into the cylinders before starting engines.

26. James Brady's 831st B.S. crew dons flight gear before entering their plane.

27. Lt. Colonel Richard Griffin, 830th B.S. commander, taxis for take-off on Nov. 5, 1944, the group's 100th mission.

28. The control tower announces clearance for take-off with a signal flare and the planes take off at 30-second intervals, leaving little margin for error.

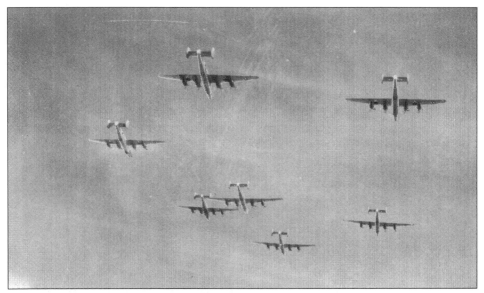

29. The planes circle, first forming into 3-plane elements and then into larger boxes, and finally into group formation.

30. When the planes enter enemy territory they are joined by their "Little Friends". Here a P-38 passes alongside the formation.

31. On most missions the 485th flew over rugged mountain ranges while enroute to their targets. The planes struggled to gain altitude, carrying a full bomb load.

32. A gunner scans the skies for enemy fighters.

33. The German air defense system was excellent. Anti-aircraft gunners had ample warning to prepare for the air attack and were usually waiting for the bombers.

34. It took several hours for the group to reach the target.

35. The anti-aircraft guns search for the groups range at the beginning of the bomb run.

36. The intensity of the flak increases as the group continues on its run to the target.

37. The lead bombardier releases bombs and the other planes drop on his cue.

38. Strings of bombs fall on the target.

39. The group is joined by another group of "Little Friends," P-51's that will escort them home. This one is "Jurldine" from the 332nd Fighter Group.

40. The group heads for home, gradually descending from altitude.

41. *Flak Shak*, an 831st B.S. plane, lands at Bari with several wounded aboard, including tail gunner Bob Hickman, who was severely wounded in a fighter attack. (Note holes and missing top of tail turret).

42. Venosa field-a welcome sight.

43. *Tail Heavy* has its gear down, preparing to land.

44. This battle-damaged 831st B.S. plane made it home safely.

45. This happy 830th B.S. crew completed another successful mission on *LIFE* and flew the plane's 100th mission.

46. The ground personnel inspect for damage. It wasn't difficult to spot the damage to this plane.

47. The Red Cross supplies donuts and coffee to the men before debriefing.

48. The crews at debriefed concerning significant events on the mission.

49. Some of the men who aren't too tired after the long mission relax in the evening. These men are officers in the 831st Squadron, joined by Colonel Tomhave (standing near the center of the photo with leather jacket).

A Different Enemy Strikes

We were not equipped for this snow, mud and cold in "sunny Italy". Since we couldn't fly, we were given all sorts of extra assignments, such as latrine and K.P. duty. I didn't mind helping out on the flight line, but I hated some of the other duties. Besides that, we were wet and cold. Try as we might to maintain our tent, there were still leaks and a danger of collapse from the snow. Morale in the group, normally pretty high, was sagging from the inactivity.

January 7, 1945

Dear Mother,

The weather has been too poor to fly. Argie got a letter to-night with the clipping of him being over here and I see our Group Commanding Officer (Colonel Tomhave) is from Montevideo, Minnesota. This was news for me. I'll have to get in good with him. Maybe I can come back a Tech Sergeant... ha-ha.

We went to a training film this afternoon at our theater or rather "Grant's Tomb", which is what we call it. Our navigator, Lt. Suttkus, is here now. He just censored some letters for the boys in my tent. He will get this one also. He is visiting with the boys now. He just came from evening church.

There was a mission on the 8th, but we weren't on it. One of the bombers from the 830th Squadron crashed on the field after taking off, killing four crew members. The other six parachuted safely. It didn't help morale any when this sort of thing happened. It was too close to home.[1]

We were scheduled for a practice mission on the 9th, but the weather was too miserable to fly. We got some good news on this date. Lt. Blood and some of his crew had returned from Yugoslavia, having been rescued by the Partisans. Captain Johnson returned with them. Tamraz hadn't made it back with Blood, but it was rumored that the entire crew had made it safely to the ground. Details were somewhat sketchy, but we heard that Tamraz and others were hiding out with the Partisans.

On the 10th, we had another big snow storm. We tried to make the best of things. As much as we hated combat, it was almost preferable to all this waiting and menial tasks. If it wasn't snowing, it was foggy and raining.

I went down to the club during a snowstorm. I figured I might as well be in a real building. I think Argie was helping out at the bar that night and I was enjoying myself, drinking "gin and juice" as we called it. I must have started early and stayed late. I don't remember much about how the night ended, but the rest of the crew seems to have a vivid recollection of what occurred. I guess I left before the bar was closed down. Argie later walked back through the snowstorm. When he got to the tent he noticed I wasn't there.

Argie woke up the rest of the guys in the tent and asked if they had seen me. They hadn't, so fearing the worst, a search party was organized. They bundled up, got their flashlights and retraced the path to the Enlisted Men's Club. There was no sign of me and the storm had worsened. The snow was coming down heavily.

50. Wayne at the latrine, when he did have toilet paper (January 1945).

According to what some of them later said, they were pretty worried. At least that's what they later told me. They kept looking, retracing the path to the club. Finally, Miller and Argie saw a very faint, pink glow in a snow drift. They couldn't figure out what it was, so they approached the snow drift and started brushing away the layers of snow. As they brushed away the snow the glow became brighter. After brushing away several inches of snow, they came to the source of the glow.... my right angle flashlight with a red lens, grasped in my hand. After a little more serious digging they uncovered me, face up, sleeping. They managed to get me back to the tent. Miller always thought that they should have given my flashlight some kind of award for saving my life. I felt miserable the next day and just wanted to forget the whole thing. I'm still trying to live that one down.

January 13, 1945

Dear Mother,

I haven't wrote lately because I had been figuring on writing as soon as I received a letter, but have given up hopes of ever getting any mail. It seems years since I have gotten any mail.

Boy, this place is sure getting chicken. When I first came here they treated us flying personnel pretty nice, but lately, because the weather hasn't permitted us to fly, they give us K.P., guard duty, or working on the line. Guys have gotten a full week straight of K.P. duty because they didn't have any overshoes and they wore their flying boots to keep from getting pneumonia. So you can see how chicken they are getting. They make one so mad he just doesn't much care about anything anymore. It's a good thing I haven't got any shells for my .45 pistol, because I'm getting just about that disgusted with things over here.

I haven't flown since the 29th of last month. Our upper gunner is expecting a pass to go to Rome to see his cousin. Things are really rough here now. We can't even get toilet paper anymore and we don't get very many newspapers, so we are just out of luck all the way around. I stood mail call and, as usual, there wasn't any (mail) for any of our crew members again.

I see we are scheduled to fly in the morning, if weather permits. I hope it does. Baker told me about it when I was going from the mess hall to the mail room.

The weather on the 14th was lousy and we couldn't fly our mission. There was always tension before a mission, and I felt relieved, disappointed and frustrated all at the same time, when I learned the mission was canceled. The supply situation at our base was not good. I'm sure the weather affected the supply chain, but it was pretty miserable when we couldn't even find a newspaper to use as toilet paper.

51. Hazen Suttkus, Jim Scheib and Dick McLawhorn in the mud.

January 14, 1945

Dear Mother,

Another day has gone and I didn't get any mail again. I'm getting used to it now, been so long since I got any mail, so I am beginning to just live for chow and my sleep, where I did have mail to live for. All the rest got mail, but me, as usual.

I almost resented the other guys getting mail when I didn't get any. They did share news, though, so it wasn't a total loss. A mission was scheduled for the 15th, then canceled due to rain and fog.

I tried to keep busy and spent many evenings in the Enlisted Men's Club. A couple of days later, the weather started to clear.

January 18, 1945

Dear Mother,

Today was a pretty nice day for here. The sun shone for once. I believe the last time I saw the sun was up above the clouds, and I think that was the 29th of December. I hope the weather stays good for a while, now, so we can do some work again. You know what I mean by work. Boy, is it muddy out now! The snow is about all gone around camp from it raining.

There was a mission to Zagreb, Yugoslavia, on the 19th, but we weren't on it. They all made it back safely. We got to fly again on the 20th and from the way it went, I wished we had been weathered in. Our target was the marshaling yard at Linz, Austria.

When we climbed to altitude, the cold was almost unbearable. Miller had a thermometer at his station. He said it was -62 degrees. I also managed to get a thermometer and mine read -65 degrees in my turret. That was without the wind chill factor from all the wind blowing back through the plane! The heated flying suits didn't begin to protect us from this kind of cold. We had a substitute navigator on this mission. It was his first mission and they wanted him to fly with an experienced crew. He was 2nd Lieutenant Phil Stone.

Argie got his hands badly frostbitten and Nauman got his ears frostbitten. Lt. Stone had a malfunction with his oxygen system and passed out. The navigator was alone at his station, since the bombardier, McLawhorn, was up on the flight deck. Stone hadn't been heard from for several minutes and didn't answer on the intercom, so Baker sent McLawhorn down to check on him. Mac found Stone unconscious, with his gloves off. Mac got oxygen to him and Stone regained consciousness. After we landed, Stone showed Scheib his hands. The fingertips on both hands were black.

52. Lt. Phil Stone

To top it off, we hit intense flak over the target. I assumed my usual position, making myself as small as possible. We were hit several times by flak, but not in critical places. Altogether, sixteen planes from our group received flak damage that day. Only five were undamaged. I don't know if it was the extreme cold, gripping fear, or simply Nature's calling, but I felt an immediate need to urinate after we rallied off the target. I saw no fighters in the area, so I made a decision to relieve myself. This was not something Baker would approve of over enemy territory, but I really had no choice.

I slid back out of the turret, unbuckling my flak vest as I did so. There was a "relief tube" just outside of my turret. It consisted of a metal funnel with a tube on it, leading out the bottom of the plane. I stood up, undoing my coveralls, heated flying suit and underwear. I stood over the funnel, taking care of business, when we hit turbulence. My penis hit the funnel and stuck to it! Oh my God, what do I do now? I had no choice but to pull myself free,

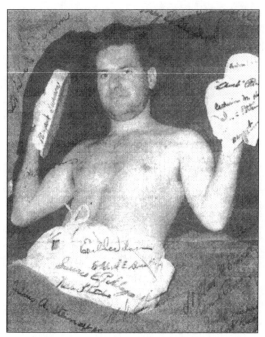

53. Lt. Stone showing injured hands in the hospital.

leaving a strip of fragile skin on the funnel. God, it hurt, but I had to get bundled up quickly and get back in the turret. For me, the remainder of the mission was uneventful, but painful, very painful.

As it turned out, three of our aircraft ditched in the Adriatic Sea. In addition, one aircraft landed at Vis and another crash-landed at Madna, a field farther to the north. **(See Appendix C for additional information.)**

Lt. Stone was hospitalized. We all felt bad about it. Most of our crew visited him at the hospital. Parts of seven of his fingers were later amputated and his first mission was also his last. His misfortune bothered all of us. Stone, Argie and Nauman received Purple Heart medals for their injuries. Captain Johnson, the Flight Surgeon, wanted to put me in for the Purple Heart, but I refused. This was not the sort of injury one wanted recognition for. I needed more than my one shot of whiskey to relieve me of the pain of this mission. As it was, I was in pain for quite a while.

January 23, 1945

Dear Mother,

Our ball gunner went to the hospital this morning. He is up for the Purple Heart, as the last mission we flew, which was on the 20th of January, he got his hands frostbitten. He went to the hospital, as he has pharyngitis now.

I heard this morning the Russians have taken a place where I put in five of my missions, so thank the Lord we won't have to go back there. We had another snow storm several days ago and yesterday was like a Minnesota blizzard. Oh yeah, three of our crew are to receive the Purple Heart. The order did go through. I was on guard last night at headquarters. It has been snowing, raining, and a strong wind here lately.

The Russians had finally taken Blechhammer in their push toward Berlin. This was a big relief for all of us. This was one place we didn't want to visit again.

NOTES AND REFERENCES

1 The pilot of the plane was Lt Charles Shackleford. Shackleford successfully bailed out, along with William Pickerson, copilot; Burton Gibson, navigator; Thomas Braud, bombardier; Harley Grill, flight engineer, and Lester Povlich, gunner. Gunners Charles Frame, Thomas Ryan, Eugene Lester and Chauncey Lyons were killed in the crash. This info is from Aircraft Accident Report 45-1-8-512.

Better Weather

We flew on the last mission of the month, January 31st. The target was the Moosbierbaum Oil Refinery, in Austria. This mission was uneventful, unlike the last one. We bombed by radar. Flak was very light and below and behind the Group, for the most part. We didn't find any holes in our plane after the mission, at least no big ones. We didn't always count the holes in our ship after missions. Sometimes we'd count the big ones in the fuselage, but we weren't really too interested in spending a lot of time after a mission doing this, particularly since it just reminded us of our vulnerability. I'm certain there were times we didn't know we'd been hit by flak. If we didn't see any large holes, they didn't count.

As I gained experience I was able to pick out the good pilots, if they were flying behind us. The good ones flew nice, tight formation. They were able to keep their planes in tight formation at all times. The pilots who weren't so good had difficulty flying tight formation. One minute they'd be in close on their element leader and the next they'd be hundreds of yards out. Then they'd zoom in again. There were several mid-air crashes in the group. Those not associated with combat, mechanical failure or weather conditions were a result of the lack of skill of a few pilots. This is one of the reasons I didn't volunteer to fly with other pilots. Some of the pilots who had difficulty flying tight formation weren't necessarily the new pilots, either.

The weather began to improve in February. Ground Hog Day was special for us because we got to take a shower, our first in a month. There was a 55-gallon drum of hot water on a raised platform. There was a hose coming out of the bottom of the drum with a spigot on it. We got to stand under the drum for a couple of minutes. We barely had time to get clean, but it felt good. It also smelled better in the tent, with six cleaner bodies inside.

February 4, 1945

Dear Mother,

I won't be able to write much of a letter as I am sorta nervous in the service tonight, for no reason at all. We were scheduled to fly this morning and they got us up at 4:30 and we waited to fly 'til 9, then they said we could come back to the tent. It was very foggy.

We went to Regensburg, Germany, on February 5th, after experiencing bad weather for a few days. Our target was the oil storage facilities there. We heard there was a lot of flak at Regensburg. We were in flak for about 3 minutes over the target, but took no noticeable hits. I had expected it to be a lot worse. There were apparently enemy aircraft in the area, but I didn't see any. We heard that another bomb group was attacked by fighters, but the only fighters I saw were our "friendlies", P-38's and P-51's. We bombed by radar and couldn't see whether or not we hit the target.

It seemed that we didn't get as much flak when we bombed by radar. The most likely reason for this was that we only bombed by radar when the weather was bad and we couldn't see the target. The Germans couldn't see us either, so unless their flak was radar-guided, it usually wasn't really accurate.

February 6, 1945

Dear Mother,

We were scheduled to fly day before yesterday, but the weather was too poor, so we didn't. But we did yesterday. No doubt you heard about yesterday's raid over the radio. We went up to Regensburg, Germany and did we go! I wish you could have seen it. It was really a sight. It wasn't bad, though, I didn't think. I can take 22 more just like the last one. Well, I have my 13th in now. I was sorta sweating that one out, as it could have been much worse.

I think I will be scheduled to fly tomorrow if our pilot gets ungrounded. He was grounded last night on account of a cold. Our ball gunner is 3 missions behind us now and the upper gunner is 2 behind us. He (Hosier) hasn't got back from Rome yet, from his 3-day pass. He's been gone 10 days now. I expect he will be a private when he gets back.

Hosier got back a few days later from his extended leave, but nothing ever happened to him for overextending his pass.

We flew another mission on February 7th, to the oil storage facilities at Pola, Italy. This target was along the coast, at the north end of the Adriatic Sea, near the Italian/Yugoslav border. Since it was along the coast, we wouldn't be over enemy territory for very long, just long enough to make a bomb run. It was going to be a milk run, or so we thought.

We were flying in a newer model B-24, an "L" model. It had a different sort of tail turret than I had flown in before. It had a "stinger" style turret. There was more visibility and the turret was lighter, but not fully power operated. Although I didn't particularly care for the turret, it was nice flying in a newer airplane.

We learned at briefing that the 485th would be the only group bombing Pola, so we wouldn't be joining up with any other groups. We were going to bomb in two separate attack units. We'd be part of the first unit, made up of 21 planes. We didn't have any fighter escort, because it was doubtful that the German fighters would venture this far south.

We were flying in the #4 or slot position, directly behind and below the bomber leading the formation. A crew that we had trained with at Boise was in the #3 position, in front of us and on our left. This was Lt. Ken Wydler's crew. We'd gotten to know them at Boise and we came overseas together. I'd occasionally see the gunners on the flight line and in the Enlisted Men's Club.

When we were over the target I saw a couple of flak bursts below and behind us. The gunners were quick to find our range. I heard and felt the explosions all around us. They were in 3-shot bursts. I was being bounced around violently in the turret. I felt the tail of the plane raise up, then fall back down and I could smell the cordite. I heard a clanging noise on my steel helmet. I looked out and saw my right .50 caliber machine gun barrel had been hit and the barrel was pointing at an awkward angle. When I looked down, there was a large hole in the floor between my legs. We had taken quite a flak hit.

At about the same time I saw something that looked like a sack of potatoes go flying by on my right. I didn't know it at the time, but it was Lt. Don Swenson, the navigator from Wydler's crew, who had been blown out of his plane. Baker called and asked if I was all right in the tail. I answered that I was fine, but one of my guns was out of commission. Some of the crew later said the tail of the plane raised about 10-15 feet. There must have been a flak burst directly beneath the tail.

I saw Wydler's plane leave the formation on my right, going down. I didn't see it crash, but I assumed it did. Of the 21 planes in our attack unit, eleven of us received flak damage. We were only in range of the flak for about two minutes, but it was very

54. Lt. Ken Wydler's crew. Front (L-R) Mike Goglia, Niran Kellogg, Don Swenson and Ken Wydler. Back (L-R) Phil Williams, Elmer Gibson, Robert Espenshade, Harvey Altman, Harold Suess and George Estok.

accurate. Those gunners were good. Our plane didn't receive any damage that kept it from flying. Colonel Atkinson, our squadron commander who led the first attack, had about 200 flak holes in his plane, but he also made it back safely. We counted only eight in our fuselage, but it had been much too close for comfort. I particularly didn't like the matching holes in the tail turret, one in the bottom, the other in the top. The entire second attack unit, bombing from 2000 feet higher with 19 planes, received no damage at all.

Wydler's plane was flying on the left wing of the squadron commander when it was hit. Baker and Scheib were both looking off to their left, in the direction of Wydler's plane, when it took a direct hit in the nose. Both sensed a body falling out of the nose. Scheib later told me he was surprised the body didn't hit our left wing. It was that close! We were one of the first to land back at

Venosa, since we were near the front of the attack unit. We were on the ground, lamenting the loss of our buddies on Wydler's crew, as the remainder of the group landed.

Shortly after the last plane landed we saw another plane approaching the field, coming in high. It was Wydler's plane! All of a sudden all four engines stopped and the plane dropped near the end of the runway. Before it hit the ground all the engines came to life again and the pilots gained control and landed. The hydraulics were shot out and the plane used up the entire runway, stopping at the very end.

Several of us got a ride to the end of the runway. Bob Espenshade, the nose gunner, was standing by the nose of the plane. I saw a huge hole in the nose, right behind Espenshade's turret. From talking with the crew we pieced together what had happened.

Wydler's plane took a direct hit inside the nose compartment. An 88-millimeter shell exploded when it made contact with the plane. Swenson was seated at the navigator's table and was blown out the huge hole in the floor. One look inside his compartment left no doubt in my mind that he was killed instantly, before he was blown out. It was an awful sight. The concussion knocked both pilots unconscious, the cockpit windows were blown out, and the plane went into a dive. The bombardier had been farther back in the plane and would have undoubtedly been killed had he been in the nose.

The pilots, Ken Wydler and Mike Goglia, both regained consciousness during the dive and were able to pull the plane out of a dive, several thousand feet below the formation. Espenshade, badly shaken, was trapped in the nose. His turret glass was shattered and air was rushing into his turret. His oxygen was shot out, as well as communications. He stood up in his turret, signaling to his pilots that he was OK. He also pointed to his mouth, signaling that he had no oxygen, a sign for the pilots to descend to a lower altitude.

55. Ken Wydler and Mike Goglia inspect damage to their plane, while Bob Espenshade looks down from the astrodome.

Somehow the pilots managed to fly the crippled bomber back to base. The hydraulics were shot out and the flight instruments weren't functioning. The engineer was able to crank the wheels down and lower the flaps manually when they approached our field. Attempts to get Espenshade out of the nose before landing were unsuccessful, because the entire floor in the nose was blown away. He had no parachute in his turret, so he couldn't bail out. They had to land with him in the turret. This was not a safe place to be, especially with the possibility that the entire nose could collapse upon landing.

During its final approach, a fire started in the plane. The engines briefly stopped, then started again, and the plane landed safely. We were saddened to learn of Swenson's death, but we were very happy the rest of the crew made it back safely.

Espenshade said he shut his eyes while landing and later described getting out of the turret as the happiest day of his life. Small wonder!

I don't know how the pilots and Espenshade escaped from being hit by shrapnel. Espenshade's only injury was a cracked rib. It was as close to a miracle as anything I've ever seen. A few days later their crew was sent to rest camp. After that episode they needed a rest. It wasn't of much consolation, but it looked like we got about 50 hits on the target and started some fires in the oil storage areas.

The next day we weren't scheduled for a mission, so we hopped a ride on a truck to Cerignola, a nearby town. It felt good to get away from combat and away from our base, even if just for a little while.

February 9, 1945

Dear Mother,

The reason I didn't write night before last was this: we had been on a mission that day which was quite rough and I didn't think I would be able to write a decent letter at all, so thought I would wait 'til yesterday.

Miller, Manfrida, and myself got a pass 'til 11 last night and went to a town about 25 miles from here. We had quite a bit of fun. They have a pretty nice Red Cross club there, so we really had a good day of entertainment for over here.

Well, I have in 14 sorties now, equal to 25 missions. I have flown the 5th of February and the 7th of February, only two so far this month, and also a practice mission. I have made all of those sorties OK, so don't worry about me. Of course, I have to knock on wood every time. I say this; some of them have been rough and others not so bad. The last one was real rough. I think I will fly tomorrow if the weather permits.

Our bomb group, I hear, has gotten a Unit Citation for a raid on Vienna, Austria, last June. I think we should get one for our raids over Blechhammer, Germany, as I think we deserve one. But, of course, we aren't the big shots in Washington. One of my guns was chipped by a piece of flak on my last mission.[1]

The next mission we were able to fly was on the 13th, to the Vienna South Goods Depot. Vienna was the second most heavily defended target in Europe. (Suttkus still remembered, 55+ years later, that there were 509 flak guns in the area.) The 485th had lost a lot of good men in previous attacks on Vienna, so there were loud groans when the curtain came off the target map. Miller had been trained as a Panther Operator and this would be his first mission as such.[2]

Panther was a code name for a radar-jamming device that was carried on a few B-24's, the purpose being to jam the signals on the radar-controlled German flak batteries. As previous experience had shown, the Germans were very accurate with many of their flak batteries, and this was one way to try to combat it. The device would search out the frequency of the radar, then jam it. As soon as this happened the Germans would switch to another frequency and the Panther operator would try to locate this frequency and jam it. The jamming device was usually positioned in a plane that flew in the slot position, in the center of the formation.

The other method we used was dropping "chaff" or "window". This was thin strips of foil, dropped out of a few planes, in hopes that it would throw off the German anti-aircraft radar.

We assembled with the rest of the 55th Bomb Wing. This time we were the third group in the formation. We had about 40 P-51's that escorted us to the target. I thought I saw several ME 109's way off in the distance, but I couldn't be certain. I swung my turret around and trained my guns on them, just in case. If they were enemy planes, they made no attempt to attack us. We heard the Germans would sometimes send up fighters and have them determine the altitude of the bomber formations and radio this to the big guns on the ground.

We were in some pretty heavy flak for about five minutes. It was initially behind us as we started on the bomb run, but caught up to us over the target. I could see the bursts as they got closer and closer. I don't recall taking any hits and our group suffered no losses. It was a relief to come back from such a heavily defended target relatively unscathed. The reports later indicated that our bombs missed the target by about a mile, but fell on a nearby industrial area.

Our next mission was on February 15th, to Wiener Neustadt Main Station, in Austria. There was complete cloud coverage, so bombing was done by radar. There was no flak at all, most likely due to the clouds. The complete lack of flak was unusual for a target in Austria, but we didn't complain. It was a welcomed relief. We were flying *Tail Heavy* again. I liked this old bomber. It was always reliable for us. The only excitement occurred when Hosier was testing the guns in his upper turret and one wouldn't stop firing. He finally got the runaway gun under control, but it created a few tense moments. It was pretty funny after the fact. The entire group made it back to base safely.

Around this time we got some good news. We heard that Tom Tamraz and Lew Baker, from Blood's crew, had returned from Yugoslavia. Their entire crew was now safely back in Italy. I saw Tamraz later, after he was released from the hospital. He had been through a lot, but he seemed to take it all in stride. Over a few drinks he told us the story of what happened to him.

NOTES AND REFERENCES

1 An examination of this letter reveals several words crossed out and the handwriting wasn't as neat and as horizontal as in most letters, rather obvious signs of stress.

2 Some of the airmen had doubts about the effectiveness of Panther. Some airmen even believed that Panther attracted the radar-aimed guns.

Escape from Yugoslavia

A round this time we received some good news. We heard that Tom Tamraz and Lt. Lew Baker, from Blood's crew, had gotten back from Yugoslavia safely. Their entire crew was now safely back. I got to see Tamraz later, after he was released from the hospital. He had been through a lot, but he seemed to take it all in stride. After being loosened up by a few drinks in the Enlisted Men's Club, he told us the story of what happened to him. He had been the upper turret gunner on *Hell's Angel*.

On the morning of the 26th of December, Lt. Blood's crew had gone through the same routine as the rest of us. They were a crew who hadn't flown much together and for some it was their first trip to Blechhammer. For a couple of the men, it was their first mission. One difference for them was that Captain Johnson, the flight surgeon, decided to ride along.

The crew was an interesting one, made up from various other crews. Lt. David Blood had originally been the copilot on Lt. Abbott's crew and arrived in Venosa in September. He had several missions to his credit. The copilot, Lt. Lewis Baker, was one of the few original crew members still at our base. He had suffered a nasty flak wound in his right shoulder on the June 9th mission to Munich, and had only recently started flying missions again. He was small in stature and quiet, a real contrast to the big, gregarious Blood.

This was the first mission for the navigator, Flight Officer George Benedict. It was also the first mission for Flight Officer Eugene Cogburn, the bombardier. Both were from Lt. Eugene McCarthy's crew and were flying their first mission with an experienced pilot.

Tom Tamraz was the upper turret gunner. He and Warren LaFrance, the ball turret gunner, were transfers from the 44th Bomb Group, 8th Air Force.[1] The day didn't start out real well for them. When they tried to take off they weren't able to get sufficient speed on the downhill take-off run. Blood braked and aborted the take-off, taxiing to the side of the runway and stopping. He called for a fuel truck and the tanks were topped off. The rest of the group continued to take off. After the other planes had taken off, Blood ran up the engines to full power, applying the brakes as he did so. He then released the brakes and took off up hill, just barely able to get the plane off the ground at the end of the runway.

Blood was determined to catch up to the rest of the group as quickly as possible. He finally caught up to them, going much faster than they were. He approached the formation at high speed and overshot them. The pilots applied full flaps and dropped the landing gear in order to slow down. At this point the whole plane shuddered and stalled, dropping away from the formation. Blood called for the landing gear and flaps to be raised and he picked up speed again. He approached the formation again, at a higher speed than the formation. Realizing he would again overshoot the formation he called for full flaps and ordered the gear lowered. Again the bomber stalled out, dropping away from the formation.

56. Lt. David Blood

57. Lt. Lewis Baker

58. Flight Officer George Benedict

59. Flight Officer Eugene Cogburn

60. Captain James Johnson

61. Tom Tamraz

62. Fred Sherer

63. Warren LaFrance

The gear and flaps were raised again, power was applied and again the bomber approached its spot in the formation. Again Blood ordered the gear lowered and the flaps applied. This time he was able to keep the plane from stalling, raising the gear and the flaps, and the plane entered its place in the formation.

When they approached the target, one of the bomb bay doors was frozen shut and wouldn't open. This was not an uncommon occurrence. The weight of the B-24 on the pierced steel planking caused the mud to "squish" in all directions and splash up into the tracks of the rollers of the bomb bay doors. At altitude the mud would freeze and the rollers would not roll in their tracks, so the doors would not open. (When we learned about this our pilots would open and close the doors a few times after take-off, in order to clear the mud from the tracks.) The bombs were dropped through the malfunctioning door, knocking the door off its tracks.

Hell's Angel was hit by flak over the target, although not se-verely. After coming off the bomb run, the formation started its long journey back to Italy. After a while, Tamraz ate a candy bar and relaxed in the upper turret. He suddenly noted that the en-gines sounded odd. From his spot in the turret he could look down and he saw the flight engineer, Fred Sherer, looking at the gas gauges on the bulkhead. He heard Sherer shout, "We're out of gas!" About the same time he saw the flight surgeon, Captain Johnson, standing on the flight deck, tying his camera to his para-chute harness.

The next thing Tamraz saw was unsettling, to say the least. Tamraz's chute was below his turret on the flight deck. He saw Sherer pick up the parachute, hook the chute to his harness, and bail out feet first through the bomb bay. Captain Johnson also bailed out. Tamraz hadn't heard the bail-out bell and hadn't heard any order to bail out over the intercom, yet everyone was leaving.

Tamraz decided he'd better get with the program. He pulled the release cord on the seat, which dropped him down to the flight deck. He hadn't bothered to disconnect his oxygen mask or intercom cord. As he dropped to the deck he fell on top of the navigator, Flight Officer Benedict, who was also on his way back to the bomb bay. Tamraz wrapped his legs around Benedict's head, determined not to let Benedict bail out without him, since Benedict appeared to be the only one left in the plane, with the only parachute. He figured that, as a last resort, he could hook his harness to Benedict's harness, and they could jump out together using Benedict's parachute.

Tamraz then saw there was a parachute on the floor of the radio compartment, behind the copilot's seat. It was the radio operator's chute, with his GI shoes attached. Thinking correctly that the radio operator must have found another parachute to use in the back of the plane, he let go of Benedict and Benedict bailed out. Tamraz snapped on the chute and bailed out head first through the open bomb bay door. He decided not to open the chute right away, preferring to get away from the plane. Looking up, he saw three open parachutes above him.

He pulled the ripcord and the chute opened with a jolt. He was still fairly high up and looked down and saw soft, billowy clouds below him. Above him he saw the blue sky and the sun. Tamraz yelled at his three fellow crew members, but got no response. He drifted through the clouds and looking down, saw the snow-covered, rugged, mountainous Yugoslavian countryside.

When he looked closer he saw a disturbing sight, a truck convoy. It was a German military convoy and it had stopped. Shortly thereafter, he saw tracers arcing up in his direction. German soldiers were standing near their trucks, shooting at him! He had to try to get away from the gunfire and started manipulating the parachute shrouds. He realized he was traveling faster than he thought and was drifting backwards.

Tamraz suddenly heard and felt a crash. He thought he'd broken every bone in his body. He'd fallen into a tree and was hanging from the parachute shrouds. He checked his limbs and everything seemed to be working, so he unfastened the parachute harness and climbed down from the tree. He had landed on the side of a mountain.

He realized that the Germans would be searching for him and his crew. He didn't know exactly where they were, but he knew the general direction and they couldn't be too far away. The parachute would be easy to spot, so he climbed up the tree and pulled the parachute down. He buried his harness in the snow, bundled up the parachute, tucked it under his arm and began running in the opposite direction of the truck convoy.

Yugoslavia was not a safe place to be, even if one eluded the Germans. When Germany attacked Russia, the Yugoslav People's Army of Liberation, commonly known as the Partisans, was formed within Serbia. They were led by Josip Broz, also known as Marshal Tito. These were the communists. Another group, known as the Chetniks, supported the Yugoslav government in exile in London. This group was led by General Draja Mikhailovitch. These two groups initially cooperated with each other, but a rivalry developed, especially after Mikhailovitch was named Minister of War by the government in exile. Marshal Tito refused to yield his command to Mikhailovitch and the rivalry turned into a civil war. Some of the Chetniks were known to collaborate with the Germans. The third group was the Ustashi, who had allied themselves with the Germans. The Ustashi were the most dangerous and had developed a reputation for killing Allied airmen.

Tamraz didn't have time to ponder the political situation. He was more concerned about getting away from the Germans. He tried not to leave footprints in the snow, jumping from rock to rock, but soon heard the sound of stomping feet and hid behind a large boulder, covering himself with the parachute. When he peeked out, he saw six or seven armed German soldiers. They were accompanied by three or four rough-looking guys with beards, probably Ustashi. He stayed behind the rock for a couple of hours, until long after the Germans left. Although it wouldn't have been much help, he wished he'd brought his .45 automatic with him on this mission.

He carefully came out from behind the rock and began walking. He saw a valley far below. He decided to wait until dark and then make his way down to a farmhouse in the valley. He would be less likely to be seen in the darkness. He thought he could hide in the barn at the farm and hopefully spend the night there. As he was formulating his plan, he heard voices. He looked around and saw three peasant girls on a path, approximate ages eighteen, fifteen and twelve. He decided to approach them for help, figuring that he could get away from them even if they weren't friendly.

Tamraz stood up and the girls saw him. He gave the girls the "V for Victory" sign with his hand. They didn't acknowledge it and just stood there, staring at him. He asked them if they were Ustashi and they all nodded. He asked them if they were Chetniks and they all nodded again. He asked if they were Partisans and they nodded a third time. So much for communications.

Two of the girls hugged him. The oldest girl left and the other two stayed with him. It appeared that they were trying to tell him they should stay put until dark. After dark, they led him down the side of the mountain to the farmhouse in the valley.

Using sign language and a few words like "Boche", the girls indicated their parents had been killed by the Germans. They also had a six year-old brother at the house. They fed Tamraz bread and bacon and put him in a large bed, covering him with blankets and a comforter. After Tamraz was in bed, a man came to the house. Using sign language, he indicated he'd return later. Tamraz went to sleep.

The next day the male visitor from the previous night brought another man to the house. This man spoke a little bit of English and told him to stay at the house. He now knew these men were

64. Some of the Partisans who rescued Lt. Blood's crew. Standing second from left is Michael Yaworsky. Near the center of the photo, being held up by two women, is is the injured Eugene Cogburn.

associated with the Partisans, a good sign. A day or so later a group of Partisans came to pick him up. Before leaving, the girls hugged him. He gave them part of his nylon parachute as a parting gift.

He walked with the Partisans, through two feet of snow, for about a day, arriving at the town of Sanski Most. There he was reunited with his entire crew. He was the last one to join them. He attributed this to the free fall, prior to opening his parachute. He landed several miles from the others.

When he saw Sherer, who had taken his parachute, Tamraz swore at him. Lt. Blood broke them up. At this point Tamraz wasn't happy with Blood either, since he heard no announcement from the pilot that they were bailing out and didn't hear the bail-out bell. Tensions soon eased and Tamraz learned what happened to the others when they bailed out.[2]

The bombardier, Lt. Cogburn, broke his leg in two places when he landed. Sherer landed near Cogburn and went to assist him. The two were soon joined by Captain Johnson, who set

Cogburn's leg and splinted it. The three of them spent the night near Drvar. Tom's good buddy, tail gunner Warren LaFrance, injured both feet when he pulled the ripcord of his parachute, violently jerking his boots off his feet. Lts. Blood and Baker and Flight Officer Benedict landed near each other and spent the first night or two with the Partisan commander at Drvar. The other gunners, Kolvet and Gibson, and Yaworsky, the radio operator, landed in the same general area. These men were reunited and brought to Sanski Most by train, where they joined Tamraz. Cogburn was taken to the local hospital.

There were also other American bomber crews at Sanski Most, some from other groups in the 55th bomb wing, a total of about 84 men.[3] On the night of December 31st, the Americans went to an airfield near the town and began stomping down the snow and lighting fuel-filled barrels along the field, in anticipation of planes coming to rescue them. The planes did not arrive. The next morning the Partisan commander ordered most of the Americans to leave town. Food was scarce and apparently the money being used by the Americans from their escape kits was causing inflation.

About 60 airmen were put on a train, including Sherer and Tamraz. The train left Sanski Most on January 1st and traveled through the night. The snow was very deep and the train had difficulty maneuvering through the heavy snow, barely creeping along. The train traveled during the daytime and stopped at night. On the morning of January 3rd, the train was frozen to the tracks in the below zero temperatures. They were stuck. Another engine arrived in the afternoon to take the Americans back to Sanski Most. The train traveled through the night and broke down several miles from Sanski Most. Tamraz, Sherer and the others walked back to town in the freezing cold.

On the afternoon of January 5th, three C-47's landed, escorted by P-51 Mustangs. The C-47's picked up 66 of the Americans. The seriously injured were loaded first, then the others began to board the planes, according to the shootdown date, those with the earliest shootdown dates boarding first. Blood, Cogburn, Johnson, Yaworsky and LaFrance were able to board.[4] Tamraz didn't make the cut and was told he was staying, since the planes were full. Since he didn't have a gun with him, he approached the crew chief on one of the C-47's, noting the crew chief was wearing a .45 on his side. Tamraz explained he didn't have a gun and asked the crew chief if he could have his weapon, since the crew chief wouldn't need it in Italy. The crew chief refused, so Tamraz asked the pilot of the C-47 to intervene, but received the same answer.

The next day, the 18 remaining airmen again boarded the train. These included Baker, Benedict, Kolvet, Gibson, Sherer and Tamraz. Once again they traveled for two or three days, creeping along the snow-covered tracks, until the train got stuck in the snow at Srnetica. Gibson became violently ill, suffering from dysentery. They were also out of food. The men were ordered off the train, and walked through heavy snow to Potici, a tiny village, a distance of about ten miles. They spent a few days there, until they ran out of food.

On January 12th, the Partisan captain and two Partisans left to reach a town about ten miles away. Two Partisans returned during the night, without the captain. The Americans began walking through the mountains and heavy snow, finding the Partisan captain's frozen body just a few miles from his intended destination.

At one point during the trek they were fired on by German or Ustashi ski troopers. The Partisans returned fire. Apparently no one was hit and the ski troopers eventually left.

They arrived at the town of Livno on January 18th, having walked an estimated 65-70 miles cross-country, through the mountains, in freezing temperatures. By this time the co-pilot, Lew Baker, had developed pneumonia. Tamraz spoke some Turkish and Assyrian and could communicate somewhat with the locals, at least better than the others. Some of the officers asked Tamraz to stay with Baker. Tamraz agreed to stay and two other airmen stayed, while the fourteen other Americans started walking to Split, a town along the Adriatic Coast.

Benedict, Kolvet, Sherer and Gibson were among the fourteen that left, Gibson having recovered enough to travel. The group walked to Sinj, a distance of 20-25 miles. From there they boarded a train that took them to Split. A PT boat picked them up at Split and took them to the island of Vis. A C-47 flew them back to Bari, Italy, on January 27th.

While Tamraz was at Livno, a group of Partisans brought in a captured German soldier. When Tamraz saw them, the German was eating. He asked the Partisans where they were going and one answered that they were going to shoot the German after feeding him. Tamraz protested, telling them they couldn't kill the soldier because it violated the Geneva Convention. The Partisans answered that the soldier had already been tried and they didn't care about the Geneva Convention.

Tamraz tried to stall the Partisans, but to no avail. The Partisans asked him if he wanted to watch the execution and he declined. The Partisans left with the German, returning later without him. One of the Partisans was wearing the German soldier's boots and another was wearing his pants.[5]

Tamraz and Baker eventually left Livno, after Lewis's condition improved, walking part of the way and then traveling by truck. They arrived in Sinj and then took a train to Split. From there they were picked up by an American Air-Sea rescue boat and taken across the Adriatic to Bari, Italy. They were back in Italy on February 7th.

NOTES AND REFERENCES

1 Tamraz flew several combat missions with the 44th BG out of England, starting around D-Day. The 8th AF was eliminating ball turrets on their B-24's. LaFrance, being a ball gunner, didn't fly the missions with Tamraz, although they were on the same crew. Both volunteered for training in the B-32 Dominator and were instead sent by ship to Italy and to the 485th BG.

2 Tamraz got along well with Sherer after this incident, which was undoubtedly magnified by the stressful conditions of the bail out.

3 This number of 84 comes from Charles Stanley Jr., who has extensively researched the crews who were downed in this region at this time. Among these men were several of Charles Stewart's 829th B.S. crew, downed on 11/17/44.

4 Cogburn and LaFrance were injured, but it's interesting that the others were able to board the aircraft, if shootdown date was the secondary criteria, since others who had been in Yugoslavia longer were not allowed to leave.

5 Much of Tom Tamraz's story was obtained from Tom during a series of phone conversations, from his Escape Statement and an audio recording he sent to the author. While Tamraz's recollections aren't identical with others who were in his group at the time, they're very similar and tell a complete story, especially when coupled with Charles Stanley Jr's research summary 'CHRONOLOGY-Yugoslavia'.

We Lose Our Commander

We were surprised to see we were scheduled for another mission on February 16th. This time it was a familiar place, Regensburg, Germany. The target was the Obertraubling Messerschmitt factory, purported to be the largest German aircraft factory. Colonel Tomhave led the group.

While enroute to the target there was flak over an area that wasn't reported to have anti-aircraft guns. This was somewhere in the vicinity of the Italian/Austrian border. There was no damage from the flak and we guessed they might be mobile flak guns from a railroad car. Suttkus noted the position so he could tell the debriefing officers about it after the mission. Earlier, while flying over northern Italy, our pilots noted that the B-24 flying on the left wing of Colonel Tomhave, piloted by Lt. Carl Stockdale, was having trouble staying in formation. It would be in close formation and then would drift off to the side, away from the formation, then slid back in again. This apparently continued the entire distance to the target, although I certainly couldn't see it from my position in the tail.

65. Colonel John Tomhave

We ran into the usual heavy flak over the target. We dropped sticks of incendiary bombs on the factory. The target was obscured somewhat from the smoke of earlier attacks, but it looked like we got good hits on the factory complex. We didn't take any major hits over the target and no planes from our group were lost in the target area.

On the way home, as we were descending from the bombing altitude of 23,000 feet with the formation, Suttkus reported to Baker that we would soon be in the vicinity of the flak we saw enroute to target if the formation maintained its current heading. There was radio silence in effect, so Baker couldn't do anything about it. We stayed on the same heading and, as we reached the area where the flak was seen earlier, we were at about 17,000 feet. At that time there were flak bursts around us, in patterns of four, which we called "box barrages".

I heard later that the plane on Tomhave's left wing had veered away from the formation and was sliding back in when there was a flak burst in the lead group. Tomhave's #3 engine took a direct hit and the plane veered to the left just as the other plane was coming back into formation. The two planes collided. The tail was sheered off Tomhave's plane and both planes went down. I heard excited chatter on the interphone after the planes collided about what happened and Baker called out, "Watch for chutes!"

I could see Tomhave's plane falling, without its tail. It was a sobering sight. I never saw the other plane, but I heard it lost part of a wing. I didn't see any chutes come out of Tomhave's plane and was later surprised to learn that at least one chute was seen. After landing, we counted eighteen holes in our plane. One of the bigger holes was where an 88 millimeter shell had gone through our wing without exploding, missing our fuel tanks. Once again we avoided disaster.

That night we listened to Axis Sally on the radio, as we occasionally did. Axis Sally was an American woman who had gone to Germany before the war and broadcast propaganda for the Germans. She was supposed to be demoralizing, but she often had the opposite effect. Along with her propaganda, she played some pretty decent music. On this occasion she offered her condolences to the 485th Bomb Group for the loss of our second commander. In my own mind I was certain no one had gotten out of Tomhave's plane, despite the fact that others thought they had seen a parachute come out of the aircraft. I could clearly see the plane going down against the white background of the snow-covered mountains.

After I returned from overseas, I stopped in at a drugstore in Montevideo, Minnesota, seeing the name "Tomhave" on the storefront. I knew that Colonel Tomhave was from Montevideo and I wanted to tell his family how much he meant to the men in the group. I met Colonel Tomhave's father in the store. He phoned Colonel Tomhave's wife who met us at the store with her infant daughter. I learned from Mrs. Tomhave that her husband bailed out and landed safely, only to die several days later on a train carrying POWs as a result of being strafed or bombed by Allied planes. I had no idea he survived the mid-air crash and still find it hard to believe.

Only recently I learned that there were other survivors from Tomhave's plane. Three of the gunners managed to bail out. Another survivor was Major Olen Cooper Bryant, our group navigator. His story is nothing short of miraculous.

Major Bryant was on his second tour of duty in Europe. He was part of the original HALPRO detachment of B-24's sent to

66. Olen Cooper Bryant receiving a decoration earlier in the war.

the Middle East in 1942, under the command of Colonel Halverson. As part of this group he had flown on the very first raid to Ploesti in June of 1942, more than a year before the famous low-level raid. While flying out of North Africa, he was awarded the Silver Star for his efforts in bombing an Italian fleet. The fleet was enroute to engage British ships trying to re-supply the British soldiers at Malta. After completing his tour he returned home, got married and was sent to Italy in February 1944, as Wing Navigator of the 55th Bomb Wing at Spinazzola. After a few months he requested to be returned to combat flying status. The request was originally denied by General Acheson, 55th Wing Commander. He eventually reconsidered. Major Bryant came to us in January 1945, as our group navigator. This was his third mission with our group.

Bryant's last recollection was that he was in the nose of the plane, returning from the mission and found his oxygen mask

66a. Lt. Carl Stockdale's crew. Front (L to R) George Sampson, bombardier; Carl Stockdale, pilot; Arnold Mick, copilot and William T. Miller, navigator. Back (L to R) Earl Beatty, top turret; Milton Wolfson, flight engineer/waist gunner; Theo Molek, radio operator/waist gunner; John Flynn, tail gunner; Frank Grippo, nose gunner and Jesse Hall, ball gunner.

was freezing up. He sat down to clear the frozen particles from his mask. He left his chest pack parachute back by the entrance to the bomb bay, behind the flight deck, at the beginning of the mission. This was his normal procedure, because he had no intention of ever bailing out from the front of the plane. He felt it was dangerous to bail out through the nose wheel door. He intended to go to the flight deck in case of a bail-out situation, snap on his parachute and jump out through the open bomb bay.

Bryant's next memory was of waking up in deep snow on the side of a mountain. He had a vague recollection of being dragged and carried down the mountain in a makeshift stretcher by some of his fellow airmen. He was beaten up from the fall, with serious injuries to his neck and back. He faded in and out of consciousness the next several days with only spotty moments of semi-consciousness, but later pieced together what happened.[1]

The flak battery that shot them down was based in the valley. There was only one battery of heavy caliber (88 millimeter) anti-aircraft guns in the area and this was the one that got them. It may have recently moved to this area, but it was a stationary battery, not a railroad flak car. The battery was located between the towns of Chiusaforte and Dogna.

German troops in the valley near Chiusaforte saw the planes falling and crash high on the mountain. Several parachutes came floating into the valley of the Fella River. Five of them were from Stockdale's plane and the men were rounded up by German soldiers.[2] Tomhave drifted into the valley, where he landed and was captured.

Another parachute that drifted into the valley was Roy Burke's. Roy was a waist gunner on Tomhave's plane who managed to bail out. He had the misfortune to land near a blockhouse, left over from World War I, that was surrounded by an iron fence. His leg smashed against a fence support and he was immediately captured. Burke was later taken to a hospital for treatment of his leg injuries and was then taken to Germany.[3]

Both planes broke apart after the mid-air collision. The tail was sliced off Tomhave's plane and part of the nose broke off. Bryant was thrown through the hole in the nose of the plane, unconscious from the concussion of the direct hit. He fell from altitude without a parachute, landing in heavy snow. (He estimated he fell 10,000 feet or more if he came out soon after the collision.)

The planes crashed near each other, below the crest of Mount Belepeit, near the Slovenian border in northern Italy. The mountain is west of the village of Chiusaforte. German troops based in the village enlisted the aid of two Italians, Aldo Samoncini and Valentino Linassi, to guide them up the steep mountain trails to the crash sites.[4]

Earl Beatty, top turret gunner on Stockdale's plane, bailed out after the two planes collided. He landed near Ted Molek, the radio operator from his crew, near a mountaintop. There was no sign of other human life anywhere. While assessing their situation Beatty saw a dark leather object protruding from the 5' deep snow and thought it might be something useful. He walked to it and brushed off the snow. It was an airman's leather flying helmet. He began digging and stepped back, surprised, when he saw a head inside the helmet. He was shocked to see the head move! He and Molek dug frantically, uncovering the moaning, injured airman. They had found Major Bryant, wearing his parachute harness, but with no parachute. They wrapped him in Beatty's parachute and began carrying and dragging him down the mountain.

Within a short while they were captured by German soldiers, accompanied by Italian policemen. They carried Bryant to a sheepherder's stone hut, where they left him, and were forced to walk down the steep mountain to the village of Chiusaforte. They were locked in the town jail for the night, with other captured survivors of their crew.

The survival of Walter Fergus is no less amazing. He was the tail gunner on Tomhave's crew and was aware of the mid-air collision. Fergus, a 19 year-old member of an 829th replacement crew, had been in Italy since the summer of 1944 and was originally a member of Lt. Art Karns' crew. He was wounded on the September 24, 1944 mission to Salonika, Greece and spent several weeks in the hospital at Bari. Upon his recovery, he returned to Venosa to learn his crew had broken up. He flew several missions with various crews, often flying with the gunners from his original crew, including Roy Burke. On this mission he was trying out a back parachute, unusual for a gunner, and wearing the chute, instead of having to snap on a chest pack, probably saved his life.

The first sign of trouble was when Fergus felt the plane shake from a major flak hit. He looked off to the side and saw a B-24 on a collision path, the plane's ball turret being at his eye level. He struggled to get out of his turret as the planes collided. Fergus felt

67. Walter Fergus

the tail break away from the rest of the plane as the other aircraft crashed through his plane behind the wings, and the tail was spinning to the ground with him in it. He fought to get out of the plane, but the centrifugal force from the spin was too powerful. At some point during the descent, pieces of the stabilizers separated from the tail and the tail stopped spinning for a moment. He jumped, pulling the ripcord as he exited the tail. He felt a jolt when the parachute opened, followed by the sensation of swinging in the parachute, and suddenly hit the side of the mountain, in deep snow.

Fergus got up and looked around, shaken but uninjured. Nearby he saw the tail. He surveyed the area, taking stock of his predicament. As far as he could see there were snow-covered, steep, rugged mountains and he was near the top of one of them. There was no sign of life anywhere, no roads or paths, no villages or houses, no smoke from distant chimneys, no fences, no sign of livestock, just snow and jagged mountain peaks. Any sort of movement was difficult in the heavy snow and he didn't know which direction to go. He stood in the snow and pondered his situation.

He had been taught to bury his parachute, so he walked to a crevice, stepped into it and buried the chute in the snow. He turned and saw a vertical drop at the edge of the crevice. He climbed out of the crevice and walked in the opposite direction, trying to decide in which direction to go. He didn't even know what country he was in. He walked through the heavy snow for several minutes, trying to get his bearings.

Fergus saw a figure approaching him in the distance. It was Luigi Naidon. Naidon, who lived at a lower elevation, saw the planes going down and came to investigate. Fergus and Naidon tried to talk, but couldn't understand each other due to the language barrier. Fergus repeated "Switzerland" several times, trying to get the point across that he wanted to get to Switzerland. As the men stood on the side of the mountain looking at each other, several more figures approached. This time there was no doubt as to their identity. They were German soldiers stationed at Chiusaforte, who had climbed the mountain. They captured Fergus and led him off.

By now it was getting dark and Fergus was tired from walking through the deep snow. They had gone a short distance when they came to a hut. The Germans took him inside the one-room structure, where Fergus saw a man lying on the floor. The cabin was dimly lit by a lantern. Fergus saw it was an airman with severe head injuries, bleeding from his ears and nose. Fergus approached the unconscious man. He saw the gold oak leaves of a major on the shoulders of the man's coat. He didn't know him, but he didn't know any of the officers on the plane that day, aside from Colonel Tomhave. The major was in bad shape. Fergus couldn't do anything for him, having no medical supplies, but sat

68. Roy Burke

down alongside him. Fergus didn't know it at the time, but he had found Major Bryant.

Some of the Germans left, leaving three soldiers and Naidon to spend the night with Fergus and the major. The hut was small enough that it seemed crowded with the six men inside. There were no beds, chairs or table in the room, just the cold floor. Bryant regained consciousness off and on throughout the night. He seemed to be aware of his situation, but would then lapse into unconsciousness. All Fergus could do was sit with the major, talk to him and try to comfort him.

The next morning another Italian man arrived at the hut. He gave Fergus an egg. There was no way to cook it, but Fergus was hungry and ate the raw egg. That morning the group began their long, difficult trek down the mountainside. It took them several hours of trudging through the heavy snow to make it to the valley below. The guards loaded Fergus onto a truck and he was taken to the village of Chiusaforte where he was locked in a cell for the night. Lt. Stockdale and Lt. Miller both survived the

68a. Luigi Naidon

mid-air collision with Tomhave's plane and were quickly captured and taken into Chiusaforte. On the morning after their bail-out German guards took these two officers up the mountain to the sheepherder's hut and they carried Major Bryant down the mountain. They loaded Major Bryant onto a truck and he was taken to a temporary German army hospital in Tarvisio, near the Austrian border. Fergus was taken to a nearby town with Molek and Beatty and the three men were put on a train, accompanied by two German guards and taken to Germany. The officers from Stockdale's plane, which included Stockdale, Mick and Miller were later taken to a POW camp in Germany.

Burke was also taken to Germany by train, after treatment for his injured leg. Colonel Tomhave was put on a different train, where he met his fate. Five of the nine men on Lt. Stockdale's crew made it out of their plane safely. All were captured and survived the war as POWs.

68b. Father Giovanni B. Lenarduzzi

The local priest, Giovanni Lenarduzzi, asked permission from the German garrison commander to climb the mountain and recover and bury the remains of the American airmen still on the mountain. The commander initially refused, threatening the priest with imprisonment. Leonarduzzi persisted with his requests and the commander finally relented and told him to do as he pleased. On February 27, 1945, when the weather cleared, Leonarduzzi and 25 volunteers from the village climbed the mountain to locate the remains of the airmen and gave them a proper Christian burial.

A German doctor, Dr. Ernst Gross, was in charge of the hospital at Tarvisio and he treated Bryant. Bryant drifted in and out of consciousness for several days, having suffered neck, back, pelvis, and facial injuries. He eventually regained total consciousness, but didn't leave his bed for a month. He was treated well by his captors. There were two Englishmen and two Americans hospitalized with him.

When Bryant was able to move around, he was encouraged to walk and was allowed to walk around town with a German guard. He was given a German uniform for these walks. As the Allies approached, he asked for his own clothes back, concerned he might be mistaken for an enemy soldier. Bryant remained in the hospital until the end of the war, partially recovering from his injuries. In early May, the Germans military forces retreated across the Austrian border, leaving the hospital contingent to fend for themselves. The Italians began looting supplies and, on May 7th, Dr. Gross asked Bryant if he'd be willing to contact the British, who were rumored to be nearby and ask them for protection. Bryant agreed. Bryant and a German soldier left town in a staff car to search for the British. They located a small group of British irregular soldiers working behind the German lines, known as Popski's Private Army.[6] Their lieutenant, once assured that the main German force had left Tarvisio, agreed to accompany them back to town. The British set up camp near the hospital.

Bryant stayed for a few days and then decided to try to get back to southern Italy. May 8th had passed and the European war was officially over. Several days later he hitched a ride south to Udine in an ambulance, where he spent the night. The next day he made his way to the airfield on the edge of town. U.S. planes were in the process of ferrying supplies to Udine from farther south in Italy.

Bryant saw an American B-17 and approached the pilot. The pilot said he was returning to Foggia and Bryant asked the pilot for a ride back to Foggia, which wasn't far from our base at Venosa. The pilot said it was against orders to take any passengers and refused to give Bryant a ride. By this time, Bryant was in no mood to be turned down. Bryant told the pilot, a captain, that he was going back into Udine to get a gun. He was going to return to the airfield and if the pilot was still there, there would be two people not going to Foggia. After further discussion, the pilot agreed to take Bryant back with him.

By the time Bryant got back to Foggia on May 15th, the 485th base at Venosa had already been disbanded. He phoned 55th Wing headquarters and asked for someone to come and pick him up. General Acheson, the 55th Wing commander, got on the phone to talk to him and immediately sent a B-25 to pick him up and take him to Spinazzola. His friends at Spinazzola thought he was dead and were elated to see him alive. Bryant's wife, back in Mississippi, had been writing to the wives and mothers of the missing crew members and had heard from the relative of one of the POW gunners that Bryant had survived. None of us knew he had survived until more than 30 years later.[7]

Captain Richard Boehme was the co-pilot on Tomhave's plane. He was killed, along with the remainder of the crew.[8] Boehme was the Assistant Group Operations Officer and had always been very lucky. Boehme bailed out along the Yugoslavian coast on October 16th, returning from Graz, Austria. He landed in the Adriatic Sea near the Yugoslavian coast, where he became entangled in his parachute lines. He was able to get free and was rescued by Partisans, who assisted him in making his way back to Italy. He was awarded the Silver Star for his evasion and successful return to Italy.

Boehme returned to flying status and was again forced to bail out over Yugoslavia, while returning from the November 17th mission to Blechhammer. He spent a month in Yugoslavia, assisted by both Chetniks and Partisans, before making it back to Italy. On his return he was reassigned from the 829th Squadron to Group Headquarters and continued flying until his luck ran out on this mission.[9]

The radio operator on Col. Tomhave's crew, Lewis Matthews, also survived. Wind currents blew him east, to the next valley. Local Italians hid him and he evaded capture until the war ended.

NOTES AND REFERENCES

1 This story is compiled from several sources, including a video taped 1990 interview with Cooper Bryant, supplied by his family. In addition, there were 4/4/07 and 4/7/07 phone interviews with Walt Fergus, a 7/13/07 phone interview with Earl Beatty and an investigative report supplied to the author by Fabio Stergulc on 4/21/07. This report included witness information and a translated log from the St. Bartholomew's Church of Chiusaforte parish register.

2 The survivors on Stockdale's plane were Carl Stockdale, pilot, Arnold Mick, copilot; Theodore Molek, radio operator; Earl Beatty, gunner and William Miller (navigator). Those killed were, John Flynn, gunner; Frank Grippo, gunner; Jesse Hall, gunner, and Milton Wolfson, flight engineer. George Sampson, shown in the crew photo, was not with the crew when they were shot down.

3 The info about Burke is from the first Fergus interview and from Italian witness statements. Fergus saw Burke at the end of the war in a POW camp and heard his story there.

4 Beatty didn't know Bryant's name and had never seen him previously. At the time he only knew the airman was a major, from his collar insignia, and seemed to recall a name tag on his coat similar to "Barnett."

5 Although Beatty, Molek and Fergus were taken to Germany on the same train and were together, Fergus and Beatty had only vague recollections of being together.

6 This information was confirmed by Popski's Private Army War Diary records, provided to the author by Friends of Popski's Private Army Preservation Society, which indicate that "R" Patrol entered Tarvisio on May 7th at the request of the German commander, in order to protect the hospital from Italian Partisans.

7 Bryant's family also supplied the author with another version of Bryant's story from an unknown source, indicating he had fallen to the ground in the nose of the plane. Beatty's firsthand account of finding Bryant in the snow without a parachute, coupled with the parish priest's log, clearly indicate he fell from the plane without a parachute.

8 The men killed on Colonel Tomhave's plane were Richard Boehme (copilot), John Carmody (navigator), James Cahen III (navigator), Marvin Woodcock (bombardier), James Dixon (flight engineer), and Bruce Graves (radio Operator).

9 The background information on Captain Boehme is from his two previous Escape Statements, from the 3/5/45 edition of *Bombs Away*, and from *Don't Let the Blue Star Turn Gold*.

The Bombing Continues

We had a couple of days off and were on the mission board again for February 19th. The target was Vienna, one of my most feared targets. The weather conditions were poor and the group had difficulty forming up after take-off. We were in the last box and lagged behind the rest of the group. As we headed north into Austria, the group leader saw another group heading in the opposite direction and assumed that our primary target, Vienna, was overcast. There was a strong north wind and several pilots were concerned about the fuel situation. It required a lot of fuel to form up originally, because it took the crews a while to find each other in the clouds and fog. With this in mind, the group leader decided to head for an alternate target closer to home.

Our box was still lagging behind the formation. The others descended to bomb Pola, while our box bombed the Maribor marshaling yard in Yugoslavia. It looked like we missed the target. It was extremely cold again. Five of our planes landed at other bases, short on fuel. One plane was listed as MIA. We made it back to our base. I was glad we didn't have to go to Vienna.[1]

69. Lt. Colonel John Atkinson

On the 23rd we were scheduled for another mission. The primary target was the Wels marshaling yard near Linz, Austria. The target was completely undercast, so we bombed the alternate target at Bruck, Austria. This was another mission on which our radio operator, Bill Miller, served as a Panther Operator and worked at jamming the German radar-controlled flak.

Some of the guys in our group spotted a lone, red-tailed B-24 being attacked by two ME 109's. The German fighters were driven off by five P-51's. Flak was heavy over the target on the bomb run for two or three minutes. One of our group received a direct hit over the target area and burst into flames. Several chutes were observed, including one that was on fire.[2] Another plane was badly hit and had its ailerons damaged and hydraulics shot out. The crew bailed out over Prkos, Yugoslavia, and was evacuated safely to Bari within a few hours.[3]

We took some hits, as usual. It was obvious that Panther was not completely effective. In addition to the planes that went down, two planes received major flak damage and thirteen more had minor damage.

We had a few days off. Baker had tonsillitis, so our entire crew had a brief respite. On the 27th, Baker got word that his wife had a baby boy. I passed out cigars and we had a little celebration. We looked for any reason to celebrate, because we didn't find many while flying combat, and this certainly was a good one.

Our last mission of the month was on the 28th. The target was the Ora marshaling yard in northern Italy and we flew in the lead plane with Lt. Colonel Atkinson. It was a relatively short mission and was intended to be another "Milk Run". Unfortunately, it didn't turn out that way. Of the seventeen bombers that made it over the target, two received major damage and eight planes had minor damage. One of the planes in our squadron, Lt. Schaefer's, had its controls shot out, but the crew managed to bring the plane back safely after Sgt. Jim Kane spliced some rudder cables together.

February 28, 1945

Dear Mother,

If this sounds crazy just ignore it as I just got back from a mission and it was quite a rough one. I am getting sorta flak happy as is everyone else who has been on quite a number of missions.

We flew a practice bombing mission yesterday. We flew with the colonel, then today we flew with him on a combat mission. We left our copilot here and also our nose gunner and bombardier, and we led the group. We took the squadron navigator and bombardier. We are really getting up there now, flying with the colonel.

Tomorrow is our regular day to fly, so I expect we will fly again, then have a couple of days on the ground, which one needs. I have in 20 now and 15 left to go. We went to Ora, Italy today. We flew over the front lines, but were so high, of course, that we couldn't see troops.

I will try to relax by going to the show. Our pilot got word last night that he is the father of a baby boy. I passed out cigars last night.

The scheduled target for March 1st was the Moosbierbaum marshaling yard. We were flying *The Character* again. Before take-off we got the usual prayer from Sgt. York, the crew chief. The plan was to bomb by radar. The radar system malfunctioned on the lead aircraft while approaching the target, so we abandoned this target and headed to an alternate target in Austria, the Amstettin marshaling yard.

Word came back later that we missed the target and may have bombed the town of Burghausen. From 20,000 feet our bombing was pretty impersonal. We could see the explosions on the ground, but I didn't consider collateral damage or casualties. While over the target area we were in flak only for about 30 seconds. Two aircraft received minor damage and all our planes returned safely to base.

March 1, 1945

Dear Mother,

Another day has passed and one more mission behind me. I flew again today. We came back fine, knock on wood again. I am sure we will have a day on the ground tomorrow, though. I hope so. Two days in a row is enough for me and (I think) most anyone.

I think we could all tell that the strain of combat was getting to us. This, coupled with the cramped living quarters and the horrible weather, was making life quite difficult. We really needed a break. Everyone was getting short-tempered.

On March 2nd, some of the group flew a mission to Linz, Austria. Four planes didn't return from the mission. There was a mid-air collision between two of the planes in the target area. Two others were short on fuel and it was believed the crews made it safely to other bases.[4]

On the 3rd, it rained and snowed. There were no missions scheduled due to the bad weather, but word got back to us that "Yellow C", an 829th Squadron aircraft, had crashed near Pantanella and there were no survivors. I don't know if they were on a training flight or doing something else, but news like this didn't help our morale.[5]

A couple of days later we flew a short training mission. The weather was still pretty miserable, which made it difficult to fly. As much as I wanted to finish my missions and go home, I knew that our crew needed a break. The tent seemed like it was getting smaller and we were getting pretty edgy. One of Argie's buddies came over from a nearby base and the three of us stayed too long at the club one night. We got hold of some cherry brandy. We all suffered from it, but I suffered for days.

On March 9th, we flew another mission with our commanding officer, Lt. Colonel Atkinson. Scheib didn't fly with us, having been replaced by the Colonel. We flew "Yellow T", a plane from the 829th Squadron which was equipped with radar. Our scheduled target was Maribor, Yugoslavia, and we led the group there. There was no rendezvous with the other groups and our 18-plane formation headed north alone.

While enroute to the target the colonel received a report that the weather conditions were unfavorable over the target. He made the decision to attack an alternate target, the marshaling yard at Graz, Austria. We changed course and headed toward that target. Just as we were turning on the bomb run, the 464th Bomb Group approached our group on a collision course. Both groups immediately changed course and the planes were badly scattered. Some of our planes joined up with the 464th and some of their planes joined our group as we re-formed on the bomb run.

We ran into flak for about two minutes over the target. A few of the planes received minor damage and one plane from our squadron, "Blue F", flown by Lt. Warden, was severely damaged. A shell burst behind and below the left wing. Corporal Holcomb,

70. Lt. Glen Warden's crew. Front (L-R) Glen Warden, Hal Wilder, Howard Williams and Albert Neal. Back (L-R) George Frenoy, Shirley Jarrell, Clarence Foringer, Carl Spiegel, Lee Holcomb and Chris Boehm.

the tail gunner, was hit by shrapnel in his right arm and was bleeding. The bombardier, Flight Officer Cecil, and others went back to check on Holcomb. They assisted him out of the turret and laid him on the camera hatch. Cecil got morphine out of the first aid kit, but the morphine was frozen. Cecil put the syrette of morphine in his mouth to warm it. When the morphine had thawed enough, he gave Holcomb the shot.

Warden's plane slipped farther and farther behind. They were unable to keep up with the formation. The rudder cable had been shot up and the flight engineer, Sgt. Shirley Jarrell, repaired the damaged cable by splicing in a heater cord from a gunner's electrically heated suit.

Warden and his copilot, Lt. Harold Wilder, managed to fly the plane home, despite the fact that they had control of only half of the left rudder and no right rudder. They had control of the right aileron but had no left aileron. Corporal Holcomb was treated for his injuries at our field. Over 275 holes were counted in the plane after it landed.[6] Some of that good old American ingenuity saved them, along with some good piloting and luck.

The mission was actually pretty uneventful for us, aside from the scramble when we were on a collision course with the bombers from the 464th. We returned to base and landed without incident. This mission was a perfect example of how a mission could be a near milk run for one crew, such as ours, but terrifying and nearly fatal for another crew flying in the same formation. One can call it luck or fate.

Many airmen had good luck charms they carried with them on every mission. Baker carried a silver dollar he found on the floor of our briefing room before his first mission. I carried a small Bible in my pocket. Some talked openly about this and others kept it hidden. Some had rituals they had to carry out before every mission. We all wanted desperately to survive and would do almost anything to give ourselves a boost.

NOTES AND REFERENCES

1 Thomas McKeon's 828th B.S. crew was the crew listed as MIA. They bailed out north of the island of Vis. Only two of the men on the crew survived. The others drowned.

2 This was the 829th B.S. crew of Robert Ware. Five of the men bailed out safely and became POWS. The others were killed.

3 This was the 830th B.S. crew of Charles Adams. The entire crew was rescued.

4 The entire crew of Lt. Earl Pooley, 829th B.S. was killed when his plane collided with an 828th B.S. plane, piloted by Lt. Carl Langley. Langley was the only survivor of his nine-man crew. He became a POW. Richard Loudon's 829th B.S. crew lost an engine and the crew bailed out. The entire crew was captured by Germans and became POWs. The other plane reported missing apparently made it to safety as no Missing Air Crew Report was filed.

5 It was Captain August Schmidt's 829th B.S. crew that crashed near Pantanella. A recently obtained letter from an 829th crewman on a different aircraft indicates a combat mission was planned and a few planes

took off before the mission was recalled, due to bad weather. It appears Captain Schmidt's plane was one of these.

6 Some of the details are from the 3/12/45 edition of Bombs Away. The other details are from an interview with Harold Wilder in October, 2006 and from his book *Grandfather Stories*.

Finally, A Rest From Combat

A fter the March 9th mission, word came down that we were going to rest camp on the Isle of Capri. We were all overdue for a break from the stresses of combat. On March 11th, we packed for rest camp and got a flight to Naples the next day. From there we took a boat ride to Capri, where we stood in line to register at the Ercolano Hotel. Capri was a rest camp reserved only for aircrew.

This island was a beautiful place, so different from our base at Venosa. Capri had also been a German rest camp before the Allies took it back and it was easy to see why. There was dancing, sightseeing and a party atmosphere. There were also women there. We tried to take in all the sights, including the ruins of Tiberius, Castiglione Castle and Anacapri. While there, we ran into two other 831st gunners, my friend Tom Tamraz and Warren La France. Both were recuperating from their trek through Yugoslavia.

March 22, 1945

Dear Mother,

I went to rest camp at the Isle of Capri for a week and really enjoyed that week. I went to all the ancient ruins there and

71. B.W. Nauman, Wayne and John Manfrida being shown the sights of Capri with a local tour guide.

> *took a boat ride around Capri. I took a boat ride inside the Blue Grotto. I really spent a lot of dough while there but don't think I will ever regret it. We lived in hotels and ate pretty good..... had it served to us on plates, and, boy, that sure seemed good after eating out of a mess kit so long. Oh yes, I saw General Mark Clark at Capri and was I surprised! I met him on the street and before I noticed his stars I noticed his face; but as I wasn't in full uniform I didn't salute him. He spoke and so did we. Miller, Nauman, Manfrida and I were all in the same room at Capri.*

Running into General Mark Clark was one of the highlights of the trip. Since we didn't have our hats on we couldn't salute, but he didn't seem to mind. He seemed like an OK guy, for a general. After a week of relaxing, it was time to head back to the war. On March 19th, we boarded the boat back to Naples. We spent the night at the rest camp hotel in Naples, expecting to catch another plane back to Venosa. There was no plane waiting for us at Capodichino Airport.

There was talk among the crew of finding another way back to Venosa, but Baker made the decision for us. He said that they had flown us to rest camp, so they could fly us back to Venosa. He was

72. Wayne relaxing at Capri.

firm in his conviction on this issue, so we waited. It looked as if the 485th Bomb Group had forgotten about us, but there wasn't much complaining. We were all anxious to finish our missions and get back home, but we weren't at all anxious to fly combat. We ended up spending nearly a week at Naples.

One night I managed to get separated from some of the other crew members. I had been drinking gin and juice and had reached my limit long before I stopped drinking. I was walking alone through the streets of Naples, which was not a good idea, even when sober. I walked quite a distance in an unfamiliar area. I finally saw six or seven British soldiers walking together on the other side of the street. I was glad to see them and, in my eagerness to greet them, I waved and called out, "Hey, you sonsabitchin' limeys!" For some reason they took offense at my friendly greeting and ran across the street to meet me with their fists. What a way for them to show their appreciation for an Ally!

Fortunately, there was a group of young Italian men nearby. They were wearing various parts of Italian Navy uniforms, so they were most likely former sailors who had given up and been released. At any rate, they entered into the fight and I was able to crawl away, leaving my former enemies to battle my Allies. It was all so confusing! Somehow I found my way back to the hotel, not much worse for the wear.

On March 25th, after more sightseeing in Naples, we finally caught a plane ride to Pantanella, a bomber base northeast of Venosa. From there we got a ride back to Venosa by truck, to continue our war.

March 26, 1945

Dear Mother,

We flew back last night. We were supposed to be back here a week ago today, but we couldn't get a ship to come back, so it was OK. We spent from the 19th to the 25th in Naples….. had quite a time. I saw quite a bit of Naples also......all I care to see and hope maybe before I leave Italy I get to see the ancient ruins of Rome. Oh yeah, they got me up this morning to awaken the crews who were flying today and I've got guard duty all night tonight, so you can see what a squadron this is. I hate it.

The Final Push

We lost another group commander while we were at rest camp and several other crews were lost on missions. Colonel Cornett, who replaced Colonel Tomhave, was leading the entire wing when he got a direct flak hit over the target area in Austria. A mission to Vienna had claimed yet another 485th crew. Colonel Cornett and his crew

73. Colonel John Cornett (center) with General George Acheson (left) and General Nathan Twining (right).

made a crash-landing in enemy territory and were captured. This occurred on March 22nd. Within a day or so, Lt. Colonel Cairns became our new commander.[1]

After our return from rest camp, we were immediately given other duties not to our liking, such as KP, guard duty and other tasks that we considered menial. We didn't think we should be required to do these things, since we were combat crewmen. We felt there were plenty of other people who could do these duties but, unfortunately, we had no say in the matter. We had a stand down on the 28th and another on the 30th. We were becoming increasingly anxious to finish our missions. If we could finish our missions before the war in Europe ended, it just might mean that we wouldn't be transferred to the Pacific, which was something we all dreaded.

On the 31st of March, we flew a mission to Villach, Austria. We were supposed to go to Linz, but we hit Villach instead. We formed up with our bomb wing, then encountered some terrible weather. We flew through the weather for about 30 minutes and then the wing leader told our group to circle left and climb above the cloud layer. Our group circled and circled, making a total of six 360-degree turns before breaking through the clouds at 22,000 feet. While doing this, I snapped on my parachute and knelt by the rear escape hatch. I wasn't alone. Mid-air collisions were as great a danger as the German flak and I wasn't taking any chances.

By this time we were way behind the rest of the wing. Our group leader decided to bomb Villach instead. Miller felt we missed our target, which was the marshaling yards, and hit the town. The flak was very light and the entire group made it back to base safely.

In early April we had two stand downs. The first, on April 3rd, was scrubbed before we took off. The second was on April 6th. We were enroute to bomb a marshaling yard near Innsbruck when the weather closed in over the target, so we flew formation for a couple of hours before returning to base. Although we had recently returned from a long rest at Capri, the stress was still there. Stress was compounded each time we had a mission canceled after preparing for it. As in this case, the missions were sometimes scrubbed even after we took off.

We would be sitting in our plane before a mission, waiting for the pre-arranged time to start our engines. If the mission was scrubbed prior to this time, the tower officer would shoot off two red flares to let the crews know they wouldn't be flying that day. As much as we wanted to finish our missions, there was also a sense of relief to know that we wouldn't be flying. A song was sung around base to the tune of "Three Blind Mice". The title is "Two Red Flares".

Two red flares,
Two red flares,
See how they shine. See how they shine.
They shoot them out of the tower,
They blossom out like a flower,
You're back in the sack in an hour,
Two red flares. [2]

April 6, 1945

Dear Mother,

Yesterday we flew a practice mission and today we had intended to fly a combat mission, but due to weather which was reported up over the target area or rather farther north, we just flew a practice mission. So I still have a dozen to go.....doesn't look promising for me to finish in this theater now. It's OK for me if it ends that quick, as much as I do hate going to the South Pacific. I also heard that the Russians are very near Vienna. Boy, that's good news to me as Vienna was one of our roughest targets. If we guys ever get a full day off we want to go fishing. There is a stream not far from here.....probably ain't no fish in it, but we'd get away from camp and that is a big relief.

On April 9th, we bombed German troops just beyond the U.S. 5th Army front lines, near Bologna, Italy. Our ground troops placed large panels and smoke pots in front of their lines, so the front lines could be observed from the air. The bombardiers dropped fragmentation bombs on the German troops. We were in flak less than a minute while leaving the target and no planes in our group were damaged.

On the 10th, one of our group was lost to flak on a mission in northern Italy.[3] Two more planes were lost to flak on another mission to northern Italy on the 11th.[4] On the 12th, we flew another mission to northern Italy. This time we bombed Ponte di Piave, a railroad bridge. There was no flak. On our rally off the target, our box became separated from the rest of the group in heavy clouds and we returned to our base alone.

April 13, 1945

Dear Mother,

Well, this morning when I awoke I heard the news of President Roosevelt dying last night. For a while we all thought it was a rumor, but I guess it is true. That's all we heard about it, so don't know what the cause was. If it's true I only hope Vice-President Truman proves to be a good man for the job, but don't know. I haven't heard very much about him which sounds too hopeful. I think, myself that Dewey would be the right man in that office. Well, I expect that you have heard what Hap Arnold said about the planes and crews from the European theater as soon as the war ends in Europe.... where they would go. I get to stand in a parade. Our squadron C. O. is getting the DFC (Distinguished Flying Cross). I don't know what he's getting it for, as I can't see what he's done, but I guess it's all right. It has to be, as long as a big wheel is getting it. There's nothing us small cogs can say or do about it.[5]

On the 15th, we were scheduled for a mission again. This time our bomb group had two separate missions scheduled on the same day. We flew to northern Italy by way of Rome, Corsica, and southern France. Weather conditions made it impossible to bomb our primary target in the Bologna area or either of the two alternate targets. The formation leader, Major Ceely, decided to bomb the Klagenfurt, Austria, marshaling yard by radar. We made three runs, but the radar operator in the lead plane couldn't identify the target. The decision was made to return to base without bombing the target. Our plane was low on fuel, so we landed at an emergency field near Zara, Yugoslavia. This emergency field was on the west coast of Yugoslavia and held by Yugoslav Partisans. Many crews were saved late in the war by being able to land at this field, after running low on fuel or suffering extensive battle damage. After refueling, we returned to base.

The 15th of April, as it turned out, was a pretty significant day for the 15th Air Force. In a 24-hour period, 1142 aircraft struck targets in support of the U.S. 5th Army by bombing gun positions, supply dumps, troops and German headquarters on the roads around Bologna.

April 15, 1945

Dear Mother,

I flew a combat mission today and it was a long one in hours. I thought we were never going to get back, but we did. I have nine left to go now...getting shorter...anyway a little. Today I saw Rome from the air for the first time. I could see the dome of St. Peter's Cathedral. We may go to Bari tomorrow for two days.

Our commanding officer was sending out messages about the war's end. In our 485th newsletter, called *Bombs Away*, there was a message from our newest group commander, Lt. Colonel Cairns. He referenced the end of the war being near and voiced his concern about the rising venereal disease rate in the group. Most of us had gone through a series of VD lectures and ghastly films a

74. B.W. Nauman makes friends with local
children.

couple of months before and many of us were afraid of even
looking at a woman for fear of contracting the disease.

Colonel Cairns had a very specific message and warning for
the group. In his message, he said, "It is unfortunate also for you
individuals who have contracted the disease and who may be
given the opportunity to visit your families again in the near future. None of us knows what redeployment will mean to this
group, but if it does take us to the United States for a short period,
those with VD will not enjoy the visit."

The statistics in the article revealed there had been a total of 32
reported cases of syphilis and gonorrhea in our group during the
first 3 months of 1945. It was apparently enough of a problem that
the 15th Air Force was offering additional quotas in rest camps for

groups with the lowest VD rates. That was a good idea, but it was probably easier to get VD in rest camps than other places. Naples and Rome, where most of our men went to rest camp, were the two cities with the highest numbers of VD contracted. There was probably a message there somewhere.[8]

Some of the guys and I got a two-day pass and decided to go to Bari for a change of pace. It took about 2½ hours to get there by truck (hitchhiking). We rented rooms in a private home. We ate a couple of meals with the family in the home, but the food wasn't at all like the Italian food one would envision today. These were poor people in a war-ravaged country and they didn't have much. Miller always enjoyed sightseeing and he was our tour leader. We went to a Red Cross dance and returned to Venosa the next day.

April 18, 1945

Dear Mother,

I got back last night, from the two day pass. I didn't have very much fun over there, but it was a rest anyway. I was scheduled to fly this morning. All of us enlisted men and the navigator were to fly with Captain Morris, our Operations Officer, but we had a stand down, I guess on account of the weather. We are up to fly tomorrow and the copilot and bombardier will fly with another crew. I wish I could fly quite steady now and finish up, but I guess it's a wish and not their idea. There are several crews nearly finished and I expect they will fly them so they finish, and then our crew may fly steadier. Nine doesn't look like many (missions) but it's quite a few at that, considering one isn't up to fly oftener than every third day.

I mentioned being on a mission which was very interesting. Well, it sure was. I guess it's ok to say now that it was a blow to help directly the 5th Army in northern Italy. We bombed real close to the front lines. As we flew over the lines I took a pair of binoculars and looked down upon the lines and thought "I wonder how many boys from Minnesota and South Dakota were down there fighting". Anyway, I can say

75. Captain Gerald Morris, 831st B.S. Operations Officer

I am eager to go on more just like that one. It is more the type of bombing which I intended we would do, right along, but didn't, up until then. Probably will see more like it though, I think. This is my idea. I'm going to hit the sack as I may have to get up at 4:00 or 4:30 and fly the heavies.

On April 19th, we flew lead with Captain Morris and bombed the Rosenheim marshaling yard, south of Munich, Germany. Although it was a long mission, we took no flak hits. We spotted an airfield below us with German fighters on it. None of them came up to attack us. Speculation was that they didn't have the fuel to attack us anymore. Several bombers in our group had to land at forward bases to refuel, but all made it back to base safely.

April 19, 1945

Dear Mother,

We went on a mission today. We were in the air eight hours so I am rather tired. We got up at 4:30 and my days work ended about 6:30. Well, I have eight missions left now to put in. Maybe I will finish some day. Everything went fine today. If the other eight go that well, I won't kick.

On April 20th, we flew again, this time to the vicinity of Verona, Italy where we bombed the Garzara road bridge. We bombed with 1000 pounders. Again we weren't hit by flak. It was easy to see that the war was winding down in the European Theater. We heard news that the Russians were approaching Berlin. We figured it wouldn't be too long before the war would end in Europe. We were all hoping it would be soon, but we also wanted to complete our missions. The stress of combat continued to plague us and we were all tired. We just wanted to finish and be done.

We heard rumors about one of our group's pilots capturing an ME-109 Messerschmitt and its pilot. The rumors were confirmed when *Bombs Away* came out. Walter Michalke, 830th Squadron navigator, provided details of what happened. Captain Shackleford, a pilot from the 830th Squadron, with Lt. Fedell flying as copilot and Michalke along as navigator, took the group commander's B-25 to a forward base near Iesi. They went to check on one of our damaged bombers that made an emergency landing there. After inspecting the damaged bomber and determining it couldn't be salvaged, they drove to the control tower, intending to fly back to Venosa. As the men stood in the tower they saw a fighter land without contacting the tower for clearance. While it wasn't an unusual occurrence for a fighter to land there, they noted the plane made a terrible landing, bouncing on one wheel and then the other. As the plane got closer, Shackleford yelled "That's an ME-109."

All three raced down the tower ladder and found an MP. They got to the end of the runway in a jeep just as the plane

76. Dick Fedell and Walter Michalke

rolled to a stop on the taxi strip. As the pilot got out of the cockpit and stood on the wing, Shackleford motioned for him to get off the wing and into the jeep. The pilot was cooperative and did as he was told. The three airmen, the MP and the enemy pilot rode back to the control tower. The men from the 485th guarded the prisoner while someone was being found to interrogate him.

The pilot ripped an insignia from his sleeve, throwing it on the floor. Michalke picked up the insignia and the pilot kept repeating "Me no Ustashe, me no Ustashe". They determined he was a student pilot based near Zagreb. He and another pilot decided to defect and the other pilot landed at a different base in Italy. This was just another indicator that the end of the European war was near.

Michalke and Fedell couldn't believe it when they were called to a ceremony at Venosa and Shackleford was awarded the Legion of Merit for his "capture", when the three of them had virtually the same role in accepting the surrender of the pilot.

On the 23rd, we flew to northern Italy again, bombing the Cavarzere road bridge near Padua, Italy. There was some flak this time, but it wasn't bad. It was both above and below the formation, but well behind us. One of the planes from our squadron didn't return from this mission. It was Demaso's crew and we later heard he went down over Yugoslavia after having feathered two engines.[6]

We were up again on the 24th. This time the target was another bridge in northern Italy, at Casarsa. There was no flak and there were some good hits on the bridge. One of our planes didn't make it back to base, but landed safely at Zara.[7]

It was rumored that the bomb group's last mission would be our mission on April 25th. Our target was Linz, Austria, which was the same target we'd bombed on our first mission. It seemed fitting. We didn't fly *Tail Heavy* all the time, although she was our assigned ship, but we flew her on the 25th. It was *Tail Heavy's* 100th mission, which was quite a feat and a testimonial to Captain Hank Dahlberg, our squadron engineering officer, as well as to Sgt. Houlihan, crew chief and his assistant, Sgt. George Abele. It was a 7 ½ hour mission.

We bombed the marshaling yard at Linz and there was a good bomb pattern and good hits. There was also flak again. A tail gunner on one of the bombers was wounded when his plane got hit by flak. His plane landed in Yugoslavia.[8] Two planes received major flak damage. One was reported missing after the return from the mission. I watched the missing plane as it lagged behind the formation, much lower than our formation, with #3 and #4 engines smoking. I hoped it would make it back, but it never did. The planes that were hardest hit were in the first box of our formation.

We'd had our own share of problems too. After dropping our bombs, the bomb bay doors wouldn't close. Nauman went through the open doors to fix the problem, so they could be closed. To accomplish this he carried a portable oxygen bottle

77. The crew relaxes near *Tail Heavy* after our final mission. Bob Baker and Jim Scheib are in the foreground.

with him. There was no room for a parachute as he stood on the catwalk, correcting the problem.

We were all tired when we returned. We sweated out the fuel and oxygen situation, worrying that we might run out of both, but we made it. As always, Baker and Scheib coaxed the hard-to-manage bomber home.

On our return the group photographer was waiting for us. It was extremely unusual for any bomber in our group to complete 100 missions and *Tail Heavy* had accomplished this feat.

NOTES AND REFERENCES

1 Colonel Cornett's entire 11-man crew survived the war as POWs. There was a 75% loss rate of group commanders in the 485th.

2 Words to song courtesy of Jim Scheib's memory.

3 The loss on 4/10/45 was an 830th B.S. lead crew with Captain Don Gambrill flying as pilot and Major Harold Pruitt flying as copilot. Seven of the crew were killed and four survived as POWs.

4 The target on 4/11/45 was the Campo di Trens railroad bridge. 2nd Lt. Neill Rodreick's 830th B.S. crew was shot down by flak over northern Italy. All ten men survived the war as POWs. The other plane that was reported MIA was flown by 1st Lt. Don Adams. 830th B.S.. This plane actually crash-landed with wounded aboard at a forward base near Ancona. The crew survived.

5 The 831st Squadron Commander, Lt. Colonel John Atkinson, had completed his missions. Like the other squadron and group leaders, he flew many of the tough missions.

6 Demaso's entire crew survived after bailing out. Some were rescued by Partisans; others by Chetniks.

7 This aircraft was an 830th B.S. plane, *Buzz Job*. The crew returned to base, but the plane was left at Zara. .

8 This aircraft was an 830th B.S. plane, *LIFE*. Sgt. Walker was the wounded airman.

A Tired Old Girl
Finishes Our War

Only two other bombers in the entire group had completed 100 missions, *Buzz Job* and *LIFE*. *LIFE* was the bomber that landed in Yugoslavia on this last mission, with major flak damage, and for treatment of the wounded gunner. *Buzz Job* landed at Zara the day before, *Tail Heavy* was the only 100-mission 485th bomber to finish our war at home base.

It was a combination of superior maintenance, professional pilots and combat crews, and a great deal of luck that allowed *Tail Heavy* to return home safely after 100 trips over enemy territory. There were very few olive drab B-24 H's and G's that landed back at Venosa that day. The B-24H's and G's, which were the original bombers assigned to the group, had mostly been replaced by the newer, natural metal finish B-24J's, L's and M's. A lot of photos were taken that day. As tired as we all were, we posed for photos in front of the plane.

Tail Heavy's story is really the story of the 485th Bomb Group. *Tail Heavy* started out her career as a B-24H, serial #41-28834H. She was one of 582 H's manufactured by Douglas Aircraft in Tulsa, Oklahoma, and was delivered to the Air Force on

78. *Tail Heavy's* crew after the final mission. Front (L-R) George Abele (asst. crew chief), Dick McLawhorn, Bob Baker, Hazen Suttkus, Jim Scheib and Jim Houlihan (crew chief). Back (L-R) B.W. Nauman, Bill Argie, Bill Miller, Fred Hosier, John Manfrida and Wayne Whiting.

January 27, 1944. *Tail Heavy* then went to The Birmingham Modification Center, in Alabama, for combat modifications.[1]

In February 1944, *Tail Heavy* was assigned to the 485th Bomb Group, which was completing training at Fairmont Army Air Field, Nebraska, and was assigned to Lt. Kenneth Craighead's crew. *Tail Heavy* became known as Blue C, with a blue "C" painted on the side of the ship.

When Craighead's crew was making preparations to fly overseas, the co-pilot, 2nd Lieutenant Edward Hammel, was assigned to go overseas by ship, to make room on the plane for other key 485th personnel. Hammel was one of 154 men from the 485th, mostly 831st Squadron ground personnel, who went over on the Liberty Ship *S.S. Paul Hamilton*. On the night of April 20, 1944, off the Algerian coast, the *Hamilton* was attacked by German aircraft and sunk. There were no survivors.

79. George Abele and Jim Houlihan with
Tail Heavy.

The squadron operations officer and the squadron line chief flew overseas with Craighead's crew. In addition, the plane was filled with mail and supplies. They flew overseas alone. When Craighead's crew left the U.S. mainland from Morrison Field in W. Palm Beach, Florida, in March 1944, they flew first to Puerto Rico, then on to Waller Field in Trinidad. From there they flew to Belem, Brazil, and on to Natal, Brazil, before crossing the Atlantic. Craighead and other crew members noticed the plane had difficulty maintaining level flight. It seemed to be heavy in the tail. The weight-and-balance personnel were notified at Natal and they suggested a redistribution of weight, since there was quite a bit of equipment and luggage on the plane, in addition to the crew. The weight was redistributed, but the plane still seemed heavy in the tail.

80. Bob Baker congratulating Jim Houlihan
for his expert maintenance.

The crew left Natal and flew over the South Atlantic to Dakar, French West Africa, then on to Marrakech. From there they flew to Oudna and eventually to Venosa, arriving at the end of April.

After arriving in Venosa, many of the crews were naming their bombers. *Tail Heavy* was a natural for the bomber, for obvious reasons. When the plane was unloaded, a 55-gallon oil drum was always placed under the tail skid to keep the bomber from tilting back on its tail. (Once the engines were started, the bomber would right itself and the tail would raise up.) The radio operator/waist gunner, Wesley Wagner, got a photo of a pin-up girl from Esquire Magazine and painted her likeness on the bomber, officially naming her *Tail Heavy*. Nearly all the 831st ground personnel went down on the same ship as Lt. Hammel, so most of the 831st bombers had no crew chiefs. *Tail Heavy* was no exception. Sgt. James Houlihan and his assistant, Sgt. George Abele, were

81. *LIFE*, 830th B.S.

obtained from another squadron or group and remained with *Tail Heavy* throughout the remainder of the war. Craighead's crew never got a permanent replacement copilot for Lt. Hammel, but had different copilots on nearly every mission. Craighead's crew flew the first combat mission flown by the 485th, on May 10th. This was a mission to the marshaling yard at Knin, Yugoslavia, and there were no losses.

In her early days *Tail Heavy* went on all the rough missions, including at least five or six to Ploesti, and had her share of fighter attacks. On *Tail Heavy*'s 25th mission, the bomb group came under heavy attack by fighters and one of the gunners was credited with shooting down two ME 109's.

About midway through the original crew's tour, they were on a mission to the Vienna area. After passing the I.P. (Initial Point) and just a few minutes from the target, Lt. Craighead contacted the navigator, Lt. Philip Higgins, on interphone, requesting a heading back to Venosa. After obtaining the heading, Craighead peeled out of the formation and headed back to Venosa, refusing

82. *Buzz Job*, 830th B.S.

to answer on the interphone when various crew members asked what was happening.

Tail Heavy landed at Venosa and there was an ambulance waiting for Lt. Craighead. He did not return to the crew and was not heard from again. He was described as a very good pilot and particularly skilled at tight formation flying, but the stresses of combat had apparently taken their toll on the young pilot. After this incident, Lt. Homer Disharoon was assigned as *Tail Heavy's* pilot.[2]

The original ball turret gunner, Staff Sergeant Walter Dougherty, decided not to go to rest camp with his crew. Both he and Sgt. Bob Plocica continued flying with other crews when spare gunners were needed, in order to complete their missions more quickly. On August 7th, Dougherty was flying with another crew in another plane, on a mission to Blechhammer, Germany. His plane left the formation after receiving a direct flak hit on the bomb run. It was last seen under attack by two German fighters near Lake Balaton. There were eight parachutes seen and Sgt. Dougherty survived the war as a POW.[3]

83. *Tail Heavy's* original crew. Front (L-R) Kenneth Craighead, pilot; Edward Hammel, copilot; Stanley Plesnarski, bombardier and Philip Higgins, navigator. Back (L-R) Ralph Wadlington, gunner; Wesley Wagner, radio operator; Fredrick Ricker, gunner; Bob Plocica, gunner; Walter Dougherty, gunner and George Judd, gunner.

In September of 1944, the surviving original crew members were finishing their 50-mission tours of duty and began rotating home.[4] Lt. Sam Mackie's crew was the next assigned crew as the plane continued to build up its mission total.

Tail Heavy had over 450 holes in her in March 1945, when our crew was officially assigned to her. By this time many crews had flown in her and she always brought them home safely. There are no records that would indicate that any of her many crew members were killed, but one navigator was wounded by flak on the February 7th mission to Pola, Italy, and *Tail Heavy* landed at Lucerna that day.[5] We were flying another ship on that mission.

After we were assigned *Tail Heavy*, we used a bomb fin container beneath her tail in order to prevent her from squatting on her tail. When we found her resting on the container, we would put a few of the crew in the nose before starting the engines. This would bring the tail up and plant the nose wheel back on the ground.

The April 25th mission would be the last time we'd fly *Tail Heavy*, as we learned that this would be the last combat mission for the 485th Bomb Group. Since she was one of the old warriors, certainly not very pretty and with a lot of time on her air frame, those in power decided not to have her flown home. The German fighters and flak couldn't stop her, but she was salvaged by the Air Force in August 1945, and presumably scrapped. She flew the very first and very last missions and had certainly done her share.

The Final Score

According to official records, our bomb group flew a total of 187 missions and dropped 10,550 tons of bombs on enemy installations. The 485th was credited with destroying 62 enemy aircraft, probably destroying 41 and damaging 37 others in aerial combat. An additional 15 aircraft were destroyed on the ground.[6]

We lost 59 bombers in aerial combat and 62 others in accidents or salvaged as a result of combat.[7] These numbers were probably higher than some groups and lower than others. During the time our crew was at Venosa, at least 48 planes were lost due to combat and accidents. There were at least 16 combat losses on missions that we flew, possibly more. This doesn't include the losses from other groups, some of which we observed.

The planes could be replaced, but the sons, fathers, brothers, and husbands could not. I've found no record of these "statistics" and they really weren't statistics, they were our friends. Although accurate records could be maintained of airmen who did not return, we often did not know if these men were killed in action or were taken prisoner. It wasn't until long after the war ended that a more complete accounting would have been possible. By then the group had long since been disbanded. The ones who didn't return are not forgotten, though. They never will be.[8]

NOTES AND REFERENCES

1 Info from Air Force Historical Research Agency, Maxwell AFB.

2 Homer Disharoon was originally the copilot on William Lawrence's 831st B.S. crew.

3 Dougherty was flying with Lt. Richard Erhardt's 831st B.S. crew when they were severely damaged by flak. After sustaining serious flak damage, they were attacked by German fighters. The tail gunner, Sgt. Carli Dial, was killed, but Dougherty and the rest of the crew survived the war as POWs.

4 The information about *Tail Heavy's* first assigned crew, the trip overseas and history through September 1944 is from a phone interview with Bob Plocica, original tail gunner, in 2001.

5 Info from 2/7/45 mission summary, 485th Bomb Group History.

6 Recent research revealed the 485th may have flown more than 187 missions. It appears the group flew at least two "Lone Wolf" missions that were not logged, due to their secret nature at the time.

7 Info from 485th Bomb Group History.

8 Recent research indicates that more than 478 men from the 485th Bomb Group were killed while serving overseas, including those lost on the *Paul Hamilton*. Approximately 265 men were classified as Prisoners of War (POW). Several hundred were wounded in action, but there is no way to determine the exact number of injured.

Our European War Ends

Officially, I now had 48 combat missions and 31 combat sorties. I needed 35 sorties to finish. The 485th Bomb Group was officially finished in Italy. On April 26th, we learned that those who had fewer than 12 sorties would be transferring back to the U. S. to prepare for assignment in the Pacific. Those with 32 sorties or more would get credit for a complete tour and would return home. Since I had 31 sorties, I would be transferring to another group, along with most of our crew, to finish my combat tour.

Our pilot, Bob Baker, had 33 sorties and our navigator, Hazen Suttkus, completed his 35th sortie on our final trip to Linz, which was also Suttkus's wedding anniversary. Within a day or two Baker and Suttkus left for Naples. They both returned to the U. S. by ship. I don't recall much about their departure. McLawhorn also left, but I don't remember if he left at the same time as Suttkus and Baker. Things were happening very quickly. I'm sure we said goodbye to them, but we didn't exchange addresses or talk about keeping in touch.

Suttkus was the only one of our crew to complete his 35 sorties. He had flown on a few extras, due to the shortage of navigators in our squadron.[1] The rest of the crew had about the same number of sorties as me.

The rest of the crew spent a couple of days packing, getting clearances signed and preparing for our departure. We were being transferred to the 777th Squadron of the 464th Bomb Group, stationed at Pantanella. Pantanella was just a few miles from Venosa. The 464th Bomb Group was part of our wing, the 55th Bomb Wing, and we flew most of our missions with them. On the 29th of April, we went by truck to Pantanella to settle into a cold tent.

April 30, 1945

Dear Mother,

I wasn't able to write because of security reasons. I am in a different outfit now and everything is OK. I'm not very far in distance from where I was. I guess about 15 miles is all. Things are looking better all the time over here and V.E. Day, as you mentioned, shouldn't be far away. Last night when we arrived we had to practically pitch a tent and by the time we got settled down it was bedtime. I nearly froze also. I had five blankets, but it was pretty cold, even then. So today I went and checked out three more blankets, so I have eight on my cot tonight. No need in freezing, says Nauman and I, as the others laugh at us.

I wonder how the conference is coming out. I hope they have success in settling the world problems from now on, without these nasty wars. We are over here to try and finish up, but it looks hopeless, so I will just sweat it out.

Our time at Pantanella, at least for several days, was a time of uncertainty. We were sent to Pantanella to finish our tour, but none of the bomb groups in the 55th Bomb Wing flew any more heavy bombardment missions. Our pilot, navigator and bombardier had already left for home, but we didn't know what was going to happen to us.

Our time was pretty much our own. There was no training scheduled and we didn't fly the B-24's at all. Scheib found a small British observation plane at the field and took me up for a ride in it one day. I can see why he wanted to be a fighter pilot. He could really fly that thing and made it do maneuvers that probably weren't even in the book. It was a fun way to pass the time and I didn't even get airsick.

While at Pantanella, I finally got the opportunity to go to Rome. A B-25 went to Rome to pick up supplies and I managed to hitch a ride. I hoped to spend a few hours there, but all I got to see was the airfield. The plane landed, loaded supplies and flew back to Pantanella. It was a disappointment and hardly worth the trip.

May 6, 1945

Dear Mother,

Yes, back in April I was flying pretty steady. I flew five missions, or rather sorties, in seven days, but the 25th was the last I have flown and my opinion is that I don't think it is possible to fly combat anymore in this theater. I have in 31 sorties now and four left to go, but as I say, I don't intend to finish here.

Never will forget my last one, the 25th. It was to Linz, Austria, and our crew flew Tail Heavy, our ship, on its 100th mission. I have a picture here of our crew and the crew chief and assistant by our ship. I won't send it as I'm afraid something will happen to it. Will bring it back when I come, which in my opinion will be in a few months, although I may be wrong. The weather is fine here now. The sun is shining bright. Yes, we did do some softening up before the Bologna victory. I was up there myself.

On May 8th, there was a briefing, informing us the war was officially over in Europe. That night many of the crews celebrated. Some of the men started fires in oil drums, then threw .45 caliber ammo into the drums. The ammo went off, creating some pretty loud explosions. Some oil drums containing aviation gas were also set on fire. One tent near us burned down. Fortunately the exploding ammo didn't hit anyone and there were no injuries, at least none that we heard about. There were some pretty serious hangovers and I guess we all deserved to celebrate, considering what we'd been through.

May 9, 1945

Dear Mother,

I have been taking it easy since I left the old outfit. About all I do is play cards and eat, which suits me fine. I expect you folks celebrated V.E. Day (Victory in Europe) yesterday. Anyway, we heard yesterday was set aside for that.

It was rumored that we might be sent home. We were given quick physicals and our records were checked to make certain everything was in order. On May 10th, we heard that Demoso's crew made it back from Yugoslavia, where they had gone down on the April 23rd mission. They were at another base, but we heard that most of them made it back safely and this made us happy.

After hearing about the safe return of Demaso's crew, I continued to wonder what happened to the crew of the plane that went down on the last mission. They were from the 830th Squadron and I didn't know any of them. We never heard any more about them, either at Venosa or at Pantanella.

Things happened so quickly after that last mission to Linz. Within a few days we were gone from Venosa and we lost all contact with the 485th. It was sad to lose crews on any mission, but especially on that last mission. For years I wondered what had happened to them. It was 55 years before I learned their story.

NOTES AND REFERENCES

1 It was common for the navigators to have more sorties than other members on their crew. The 485th had a higher loss of lead planes in the formations, since flak batteries often targeted the leaders. Most lead planes carried two navigators. If a lead plane was shot down, the group lost two navigators, so, out of necessity, other navigators had to fill in.

Prisoners of our Allies

Lt. Joseph Cathey was the pilot of 44-50414, the last plane lost by the 485th Bomb Group on the last mission flown by the group, to Linz.[1] They were flying the slot position in the lead box when they were hit by flak on the bomb run. They lost one engine on the bomb run and feathered the prop. They were hit a second time, the flak severing a gas line to another engine. They feathered that engine and managed to stay with the group long enough to drop their bombs.

As they were dropping their bombs they were hit a third time, severing electrical wires and starting a fire behind the pilots on the flight deck. The radio/Panther operator, Monte White, was hit in the shoulder by flak. Despite his wound, he grabbed a fire extinguisher to fight the fire and was able to put it out.[2]

They left the formation and headed east, with two engines smoking, trying to make it to Russian-occupied territory. A trip over the Alps for the damaged plane was out of the question, because the bomber couldn't climb high enough to clear the peaks. They continued to lose altitude.

They passed Vienna, still traveling east, and the crew began destroying the Panther unit in the bomber, a new B-24M model,

84. Most of this crew that was shot down with Lt. Joseph Cathey. Front (L-R) Charles Dyke, engineer/gunner; Chester Konkolewski, gunner; Ray Liebold, ball gunner; Leon Wilkins, waist gunner; John Chamberlain, nose gunner and Aldo Grandini, tail gunner. Back (L-R) Francis Newton, pilot; Everett Banker, copilot; William McColly, navigator and Lt. Osborne, bombardier. (Banker, Dyke, Liebold, Wilkins, Chamberlain and Grandoni where shot down with Cathey. Konkolewski was shot down on an earlier mission.

fearing the radar would fall into the hands of the Germans. They shot .45 caliber bullets from their pistols at the unit and also attacked it with an axe, damaging it, but not completely destroying it.

A few miles east of Vienna they spotted a grass airfield. Cathey decided to set the bomber down. They quickly learned the hydraulics were shot out and decided on a belly landing, with the gear up. Cathey and the copilot, Everett Banker, made a safe landing, not knowing if the field was in German or Russian hands. The crew was met by armed soldiers running across the field. Fortunately, the soldiers were Russians who had just recently captured the field from the Germans. The airfield was near the little village of Parndorf, Austria, near the Hungarian border.

85. Monte White

The Russians were very suspicious and unfriendly, especially after learning the crew had destroyed the radar device on the plane. The crew received a wide range of treatment by their allies, everything from threats to shoot them to drinking with them when off-duty in the evening. The navigator spoke some German, and by doing so, could communicate with some of the local people. This seemed to make their liberators/captors more suspicious and the Russians hadn't ruled out the possibility that the B--24 crew might be German spies. The Russians didn't seem to know what to do with them. Lt. Cathey felt he and the crew could get the B-24 repaired well enough to fly back to Italy, but the Russians wouldn't allow it.[3]

After a couple of weeks, the Russians decided to fly them east to Kiev. They flew to Kiev via Budapest, in an American built cargo plane (C-47). The crew was interrogated at Kiev to make certain they weren't spies. From here they were taken by train to Odessa, a trip that took three days. VE Day was announced when they arrived. They were held in a camp for repatriated Allies. The camp was filled with English, French and Belgian troops, including the Belgian General Staff. Cathey's men were the only Americans among them.

While at Odessa they were assigned young Russian women as guides. The crew didn't feel completely comfortable with them and felt the Russians could be trying to get military information.

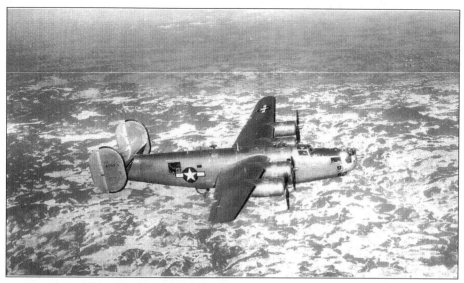

86. 44-50414, The last B-24 lost by the 485th Bomb Group in WWII on the last mission flown, to Linz, Austria, April 25, 1945. (830th B.S.)

The Russians still didn't seem completely convinced that they were Americans.

While there, the crew met a man who claimed to be an American. He spoke with a German accent, but claimed to be a naturalized American citizen, who had returned to Germany before the war began, was drafted and became a pilot. It quickly became clear that he wasn't an American at all, but a German soldier claiming to be an American in order to avoid the brutal treatment German soldiers suffered at the hands of the Russians. The Russians were very suspicious of this "American".

At the end of May, a British ship arrived to take the repatriated Allies to Naples, Italy. Lt. Cathey decided, the reasons not being totally clear, to sneak this German soldier onto the ship. They hid him on the floor of the jeep that took them to the harbor. A plan was set in motion to have the German swim around to the back side of the ship after dark, to be hoisted onto the ship by some of the bomber crew. The plan actually worked and the German was pulled onto the ship by rope.

Other refugees were smuggled aboard ship, including some Hungarian girls who were concealed in barracks bags. Odessa was filled with refugees trying to get out of the Russian-occupied zone.

The Russians became aware that one of their prisoners was not accounted for. They went to the captain of the British ship, demanding that he be returned. The captain refused to release him and the Russians ordered everyone off the ship in order to search it. The British captain still refused. It seems that some of the British sailors had gone into town the night before. A couple of them had gotten into some sort of trouble and were killed. The Russians refused to release the bodies of the British sailors until the German was turned over to them. The captain refused and subsequently left the port without claiming the bodies of his sailors.

The ship docked at Naples and the German was turned over to the authorities there. Cathey's crew was sent to another base, the 485th having already been disbanded. They were eventually given a B-24 to fly back to the States. They arrived in Bradley Field, Connecticut, on July 4th, after having been prisoners of their Allies. The crew of the last plane lost by the 485th Bomb Group had quite a story to tell on their return.[4]

NOTES AND REFERENCES

1 The crew consisted of Joseph Cathey, pilot; Everett Banker, copilot; Thomas Morrison, navigator/bombardier; Aldo Grandoni, gunner; Charles Dyke, flight engineer; Monte White, radio operator; John Chamberlain, gunner; Raymond Liebold, gunner, and Leon Wilkins, gunner.

2 White was later awarded the Silver Star for his efforts.

3 It's unknown what happened to this aircraft after the war.

4 The story was obtained from a phone interview in 2001 with Leon Wilkins, a waist gunner on Cathey's crew, supplemented by a story written by Everett Banker, the copilot, entitled *Last Mission* and newspaper articles from the family of Monte White.

Home, at Last

In mid-May we were told officially that we were returning to the ZI (Zone of Interior), better known as the USA. We were all pretty excited about that. Argie was having some medical problems, but he quickly improved. On May 21st we loaded our gear onto a B-24 and flew to Gioia, (Gioia del Colle) just a few miles south of Pantanella, to be officially processed. Processing, the Army way, took a couple of days. We were all anxious and impatient to get back to the States.

On May 23rd, we took off on our first leg home. We flew over Tunis, Algiers, Oran, Meknes and Casablanca, arriving at Marrakech after a flight of 1500 miles. The flight took over 11 hours. Our pilot was Lt. Arthur J. Karns. Lt. Karns had been in Italy since the summer of 1944, assigned to the 829th Squadron. He lost many of his crew members during the war, including several who went down with Colonel Tomhave on the mission to Regensburg. He was assigned to the 464th Bomb Group with us when the 485th disbanded. Lt. Karns had most recently been the Control Tower Officer at Venosa.

Karns could have been the best pilot in our group, but I still didn't have the confidence in him that I had in our pilots. I was

87. Lt. Art Karns

sure glad that Scheib was in the cockpit. I had no desire to fly with anyone but our pilots.[1]

Scheib had been given a check ride with the Squadron Commanding Officer, after we had flown several missions. The C.O. offered to make him a 1st pilot and give him his own crew. Scheib turned it down, most likely turning down a promotion with it. As he later told it, he felt an obligation to the crew and felt our best chances of survival were for the crew to stay together. You won't hear any arguments from me on that one.

We had to sleep in the plane at Marrakech and guard it. We didn't mind it so much, because we knew we were on our way home. The next day we took off, destination The Azores. It was cold and rainy when we arrived, after a flight of 1031 miles and nearly seven hours. We took off again the next day and flew to Newfoundland. This was a distance of 1390 miles and we were in the air nearly eleven hours. When we arrived at Newfoundland the field was covered with clouds. It took us a good hour to find the field.

The weather was so bad at Newfoundland that we had to spend a couple of days there. We took off on May 29th and flew the last leg of our trip to Bradley Field, Connecticut. The flight lasted six hours and took us 920 miles. We were all excited as we flew over the U.S. coast. Some of the guys expressed their happiness by starting to sing over the interphone. They started with "God Bless America" and continued singing until we landed. At different times various men joined in the singing. It was a real thrill when we landed on home soil again. We'd been through a lot together.

We unloaded our barracks bags from the plane, went to our temporary quarters and settled in. I really wanted to keep my .45 automatic as a souvenir, but we were told before we left Italy that we would be in serious trouble if we kept any of our equipment, aside from uniforms and personal gear. Naturally, I didn't want anything to delay my return home, so I turned it in. As it turned out, they didn't even check our barracks bags, so I could have brought anything back.

I remember going into the mess hall that night. I was hungry and hoping to get some of the good American food we didn't have in Italy. One of the first things I spied in the chow line was milk, containers of real milk. This was one of the things we just didn't get in Italy, except for the powdered variety which nobody drank. German POWs were serving the food. I picked up several cartons of milk to put on my tray and this POW tried to intervene and tell me that I could only have one carton of milk. This S.O.B. and his buddies were the reason I'd been denied milk in the first place, and there was no way he was going to deny it to me now. One of the mess personnel intervened before the war started all over again, and I walked off with my milk. I have no memory of what else was on the menu that night, but the milk sure tasted good.

We returning personnel were asked to march in the Memorial Day parade in Boston. They especially wanted to honor us returning combat veterans. I had a heck of a time getting my uniform cleaned on short notice, but it worked out and I was able to march in the parade. It was quite an event.

Shortly after Memorial Day, I received orders to report to Fort Snelling in St. Paul, Minnesota. I boarded a troop train for a long ride. After arriving in Fort Snelling, I was granted a two week leave. They wanted to send me to a nice hotel in Miami, but I just wanted to go home to see my family.

I got separated from my crew at Bradley Field. I don't think we even said goodbye, at least I don't remember doing so. I had Nauman's and Miller's addresses but, after leaving Bradley Field, I lost track of the others. Everything happened so quickly and I regretted for many years losing track of our crew.

I boarded another train in St. Paul for the relatively short train ride of just a few hours to Ortonville, Minnesota. Ortonville was just a few miles from the family farm and most of my relatives lived near there.

I still remember that train ride. The train wasn't crowded, which was nice, and not what I was accustomed to. There was only one other serviceman on the train, a young pilot. I saw the Air Force patch on his shoulder and, after a while, I sat down alongside him. He was going to Ortonville. I recognized his last name, since it was a small community, but I didn't know him. We talked a bit, but I think both of us just wanted to get home. From his ribbons I could see that he was also a combat veteran. He looked pretty tired and I wondered if I looked the same. The recently planted fields and farm houses were a welcome, familiar sight as we both sat quietly, lost in our own thoughts.

My parents were still enroute home from California when I arrived in Ortonville, so I stayed with my sister Ruth and her family on a farm just outside of town. The shortage of young men was really noticeable. Since there were no military bases nearby, there weren't many soldiers or sailors around either. I only saw a few men in uniform during my entire stay.[2]

I was very pleasantly surprised to find that one of the men in uniform was my old friend Bobby Larson. Bobby and his family lived on a farm near ours before the war, and he was home on leave from the war in the Pacific. He was an Army infantryman. He had been wounded twice, had the scars to prove it, and still walked with a limp. Bobby was a big, raw-boned, good-natured Scandinavian kid.

We were both just glad to be home and didn't talk much about the war. We spent a lot of time together at the local pool hall and liquor store. From what others say, it wasn't unusual to see both of us walking down Main Street, arm-in-arm, each with a liquor bottle. I don't remember it quite that way, but others do, so I'll have to take their word for it.

It was great seeing the family again. A few days after my arrival in Ortonville, my parents and two of my sisters arrived from California. It was a fantastic feeling, being together with them again.

Shortly after I arrived in Ortonville, I went to see one of my cousins, Marian Pratt. She worked as a waitress at the Corner Café. It seems that Esther Larson, one of the cooks, had an unmarried daughter that Marian knew. Marian introduced me to Gustie Larson, Esther's daughter, and Gustie and I started dating during my leave. (Gustie was no relation to Bobby Larson.) Spending time with Bobby, seeing other relatives and friends and dating Gustie made the time pass very quickly, too quickly. Soon it was time to board the train to Fort Snelling.

Gustie, Bobby and my family accompanied me to the train station. I wasn't happy about leaving my family and friends again. I had been told before leaving Italy that my return to the states would only be temporary and that I'd be going to the Pacific to fight the Japanese. I dreaded the thought of this, even more so now, after having heard just a little about Bobby's experiences fighting the Japanese.

I took the train back to Fort Snelling. Soon after my arrival there I received orders to report to the Army Air Field at Sioux Falls, South Dakota. That was good news for me, since Sioux Falls was less than 150 miles from Ortonville. It would allow me to continue dating Gustie and to see my family, temporarily at least.

88. Family and friends with Wayne at the end of his leave, July 1945.

July 13, 1945

Dear Gustie,

I have a good notion to go AWOL tomorrow, but I don't know if I should or not. I'm peed off with this darn army.

Even after my arrival in Sioux Falls, I wasn't sure what was going to happen to me. There were approximately 40,000 GIs stationed at the base.[3] The Army Air Force didn't know what they were going to do with all of us. I was in limbo, along with thousands of other returning veterans. Some of the airmen were going to the Pacific, some were being transferred to other bases and some were being discharged.

The point system was used to determine if an airman was going to be discharged. As I recall, points were based on such things as length of time in the service, length of time overseas, medals and decorations. Colonel John "Killer" Kane, of Ploesti fame, was the commanding officer in Sioux Falls. He had also been my commander at Gowen Field in Boise.

What I didn't know until many years later was that 485th Bomb Group hadn't been officially disbanded. Most of the base personnel who returned to the U.S. by ship were sent to Sioux Falls. During my entire stay there I never ran into anyone I recognized from the 485th. The men on our own crew were sent to other bases.

July 14, 1945

Dear Mother,

Well, I finally got my points figured out. I have 59 now and as soon as the order comes out for my other oak leaf cluster I will get 5 more. That will make 64. I only have four battle stars as I wasn't in Italy in time for one of the campaigns. Anyway, that's what they say. They say I will go to the 2nd Air Force camp in the Zone of Interior, which means in the states and be permanent party there. Of course, your guess is as good as mine, but I'll bet five to one it will be down south, most likely in the worst state in the union, which is Texas.[4]

July 14, 1945

Dear Gustie,

I sure wish there was some way I could get out of this army. I hate it more everyday. Today we processed and I found out I only have 59 points. They gypped me out of 10 points, but there is nothing I can do about it, I guess. I'll go nuts if they don't turn me loose pretty quick.

I had no real responsibilities in Sioux Falls, as yet. I was sick of sitting around the base. The inactivity was really taking its toll. I was able to get off base on some weekends and to get a ride to Ortonville. I continued to see Gustie and things were getting pretty serious. I was still waiting to be sent somewhere. For a while a rumor circulated that some of us might be sent to Albuquerque, New Mexico, as gunnery instructors, but we didn't know whether or not this was accurate information.

August 1, 1945

Dear Mother,

I am still not on shipping orders, so hope I don't go for a while. I want to try to come home this weekend, if I'm not put on shipment by then.

Boredom continued to be a problem for me. There was also the uncertainty of my future. There was still the possibility that I might be retrained on B-29's and sent to fight the war in the Pacific. I had no real assignment. On August 6th, we heard about the dropping of the atomic bomb on Hiroshima. I was hoping this, along with the dropping of the second atomic bomb on Nagasaki on August 9th, would shorten the war. I really dreaded the thought of more combat and started having nightmares about going to the Pacific. Shortly thereafter, we heard the war was ending and that August 14th was being declared VJ (Victory in Japan) Day.

August 13, 1945

Dear Mother,

The colonel said he wasn't going to restrict us on VJ day, unless it was absolutely necessary. I expect to ship real soon... might be on orders this evening, but there were too many looking. I couldn't see before I came to town, but will check when I go in at one tonight.

Gustie came to Sioux Falls and stayed with her sister, Francis, who lived in town. We decided to go out to celebrate VJ Day with Francis. It was a sight to behold. There were hordes of GI's everywhere we went. Soldiers were going around cutting off each other's neckties. We took a bus from the base into town. Everyone was drinking, laughing and carrying on. Cars were being tipped over in celebration, which was really too bad. We decided to take a bus out to The Plaza, the club where Francis's husband (Richard) played in a band. We managed to get on the bus without any problems and the bus driver headed toward the edge of town, where the club was located. Unfortunately, the bus driver was also drunk. Finally he realized he was so drunk he couldn't drive any farther and he just stopped the bus. One didn't have to worry about policemen, because most of them were drinking, too. Even if they'd wanted to control the crowds, there was little they could do. The partying GI population outnumbered the locals that night. I don't recall hearing that anyone got hurt, but the next day there must have been thousands of hangovers in Sioux Falls and all across the nation.

August 15, 1945

Dear Mother,

Well, VJ day finally came and you sure could tell it down here. Colonel Kane didn't restrict us like we had expected him to. Francis, Gustie, and I rode downtown on the bus and watched the crowd. I've never seen a bigger and louder crowd of people, GIs with neckties cut off and some of them cut off short.... their pants rolled up to their knees and drinking right on the streets. The M.P.'s were right in there with them for a good time too, last night. The civilians were also celebrating, and still are today. That sure was a great day and I don't think anyone will forget it. I got in at 4:45 (a.m.) and they didn't have any bed check or curfew last night.

NOTES AND REFERENCES

1 According to Jim Scheib, Karns was a capable, skilled pilot.

2 Some of these servicemen were guards at a POW camp, just a mile away in Big Stone City, South Dakota, where German POWs worked at a canning factory in the fields.

3 The Minnehaha County Historical Society puts the number of GI's at approximately 28,000 at any given time at the end of WWII. Since GI's were arriving in Sioux Falls and being assigned to other bases, it's possible that the 40,000 could reflect the number of GI's who had passed through Sioux Falls Army Airfield at the end of the war.

4 Wayne had never been stationed in Texas, so had no personal knowledge of conditions in this state. He was primarily upset at the possibility of moving to a more distant base from his home.

Final Flight

I hadn't flown since the end of May, when we landed in Connecticut. In order to receive my flight pay I had to fly regularly. There was no chance of getting in my flying time in Sioux Falls, but there was a base with a bunch of B-24's about a hundred miles away, at Sioux City, Iowa. A group of us were sent to Sioux City, by truck, for a training flight. This was on August 25th, and the destination was Walla Walla, Washington.

It was going to be an evening flight. Altogether fifteen planes took off, but there were only seven bombers in our element. The weather turned bad while we were in the air. I didn't have a lot of confidence in the pilots. It wasn't at all like flying with Baker and Scheib. I had never flown with them and never met them before this flight. We gunners didn't even have to get in the turrets on the flight. We just sat in the waist of the plane, passing time, to get our flight pay. It seemed easy enough.

Something went terribly wrong on the flight. I never learned whether the problem was navigation error, pilot error, equipment error or a combination of all three. As we were flying over the mountains in Idaho, the visibility decreased to almost zero. I looked out the waist window just in time to see a fireball off to the side, through the fog. It was a B-24 crashing into the side of a mountain! At the same time I heard a scraping sound and it felt like our plane hit something. The pilots pulled the bomber into a steep climb. I took a position at the rear escape hatch, expecting to bail out at any time. The pilots were lost and had to search for the landing field at Walla Walla.

We finally found the field and landed. Three other B-24's on our flight also crashed, but the crews weren't killed.[1] The scraping sound I heard was branches from the trees on the mountain top hitting the bottom of the bomber. I didn't really want to fly back with these guys, but I had no choice. The weather was terrible on the 26th, so we waited until the 27th to fly back to Sioux City. We came by truck back to Sioux Falls. It was not an enjoyable flight at all and I just wanted to get back on the ground.

The pilot, 1st Lt. Horace W. Lehman, provided a witness statement for the accident investigation:

> *I was enroute from Sioux City to Walla Walla......In front of me was R0564. We flew formation loosely all the way to Boise. Then singled out and flew air ways to Walla Walla. At Pendleton we both let down......Visibility lowered and R0564 started a 180 degree turn......I started my turn behind R0564. Suddenly I saw his wingtip (left) go down sharply. There was a red flash. I started to pull up then came the explosion. It lighted the trees all around and picked my ship up considerably. I gave full power and started climbing. At about 9000' I broke out on a 180 degree heading. Called Romeo and informed them of crash..................The waist called me and told me my left wingtip was damaged but not too bad. The engineer told me immediately after the explosion that the Bomb Bays were damaged. I called tower and landed.[2]*

August 28, 1945

Dear Mother,

Well, here I am at the home base again. I went by truck convoy from here to Sioux City where we got a B-24 and left at six o'clock that night for Walla Walla, Washington. We got there at two in the morning and were going to take off at 5:30 the same morning to come back, but the weather got so poor we had to stay 'til yesterday. We got up at three yesterday, took off at 5:30 and it only took us 5 1/2 hours to get to Sioux City, then came up here last night by truck convoy again. You most likely heard about that B-24 enroute to Walla Walla crashing, killing the fifteen-man crew aboard. Well, that was one of the planes which was with us. Four of the fifteen planes which took off that day (us included) crashed. The weather was so bad up in the mountains.

It sure is too bad those boys having to lose their lives just to get us twelve hours flying time, so they can draw flying pay. We got lost and didn't know where we were at. We were all ready to bail out several times, as we were afraid we were going to hit a mountain peak, but we landed OK and were glad to get our feet on the ground. I froze my feet and my whole body... just shook, I was so cold. All we had on was a suit of suntans and a pair of flying coveralls. I told Gustie last night that I think that's my last flying, because I value my life more than $144. I am beginning to think my number is getting close to the top of the box, and, why push my luck any more.

When I got back I checked the bulletin board and, what do you know, I am on shipping orders and my destination is 211AAF Base Unit, Sioux Falls. As you can see I finally made permanent party here, after all.

When I went to see Gustie on my return to Sioux Falls, she was staying with her sister and brother-in-law. Her brother-in-law read about the crash in the newspaper and knew I was on that flight. He was afraid I had been one of those killed and he hid the newspaper from Gustie. When I turned in my parachute I took myself off flying status. It just wasn't worth it. I thought about those crewmen that were killed on that flight, for no reason. Most of them were combat veterans who had survived a war in the Pacific or in Europe. It was senseless that they should die this way.

Having "permanent party" status at Sioux Falls was a good thing. Now I knew I'd be at Sioux Falls, for a while, anyway. I could still be close to Gustie and my family. My nerves were pretty frazzled after the flight to Walla Walla and I was still in a holding pattern.

August 31, 1945

Dear Mother,

Well must tell you about what took place yesterday. I nearly got broke to the grade of private. Here's how it happened. Day before yesterday I was in my barracks and a lieutenant came in to get someone to go on laundry detail 'til 12:30 that night. Well, he came up to me and asked me to go on it in place of someone who had shipped out on them. As I have been pulling my share I up and said to him that I wasn't from this squadron, that I came to visit a buddy of mine. So then he asked to see my pass and, of course, it was made out from this squadron. I told him I had lied to him, so he asked my name. I gave it to him, then I said that I was permanent party here and he took my name off the detail, but he turned me in to the squadron commander, a major.

Yesterday I had to report to him (the major) and he was going to bust me to private and asked me if I wanted to serve company punishment instead. I wouldn't answer him so, after he raked me over the coals for a few minutes, I told him what kind of an outfit this was, so he finally turned me loose and didn't break me or even give me any (work) details.

I was really lucky I got out of it the way I talked back to him, but he said I never earned my stripes, and I told him that if I didn't earn my stripes over there in Italy fighting, he sure didn't earn major in the states. Boy, I was never so mad in my whole life. I'll be glad when I move to my permanent squadron...think the C. O. will be better than this darn major. He doesn't deserve the right to live.

Looking back on it, I may have been experiencing combat fatigue or something like it. I have a feeling that I may not have reacted to the major the way I did if I hadn't had the close call a few days earlier on the trip to Walla Walla. I do know that he really upset me at the time. I don't know why he didn't give me company punishment (one step below a court martial), which was something he could have easily done, but maybe he felt I had a valid point.

September 6, 1945

Dear Mother,

I moved to my permanent squadron yesterday, so I am in the officer's squadron now. I am duty NCO (Non-Commissioned Officer) here.

Even after my assignment as duty NCO I didn't have much to do. There were a couple of sergeants who worked for me, so they did most of the work and they didn't have much to do either. I really wanted to get on with my life. Others were getting discharged and I was still waiting. There was no way I wanted to stay in the Army. The Army still didn't know what to do with us and I wanted nothing more to do with them, so I was just awaiting my turn for discharge.

NOTES AND REFERENCES

1 There is no evidence that other planes actually "crashed", but it's possible other planes could have been damaged by striking branches. It's also possible this was just a rumor.

2 This statement is from Aircraft Accident report #46-8-25-14, obtained from AFHRA, Maxwell AFB. It was classified as a "minor accident".

The Beginning and End

I continued to see Gustie. I was able to get off the base regularly, not always with a pass. I often went to Ortonville on weekends. It wasn't difficult to climb the fence and the base wasn't guarded very well. Gustie and I decided to get married and we set a wedding date of October 18th. It was going to be a very small wedding with only a few immediate family members present. I had to go AWOL to get married, but with thousands of other airmen at the base, I figured I wouldn't be missed. Besides, I had a couple of good men who would cover for me. My main concern with being AWOL was that my name might come up for discharge and I didn't want to miss being discharged.

We got married on the 18th of October and everything went well. Gustie's sister and brother were Maid of Honor and Best Man. Gustie's brother, Johnny Semrau, recently returned from Europe where he had been a combat medic. After the wedding, Johnny drove us to Sioux Falls where we had a wedding dance of sorts, that night, at a club where Gustie's brother-in-law played with his band. We spent our wedding night in Sioux Falls. There were lots of M.P.'s around, but they didn't bother us and never asked for my pass, which I didn't have.

89. Wedding photo of Wayne and Augusta (Gustie)
Whiting, October 18, 1945.

The next day Johnny was going to drive us back to Ortonville, but his borrowed car broke down. We had to get there, so we took the bus. There was another wedding dance for us in Ortonville, this one attended by more family and friends.

After the dance I got a phone call from one of my buddies, a sergeant who worked for me at the base in Sioux Falls, saying that it looked like my number might be coming up for discharge. I decided I should get back to the base. The whole family accompanied me to the bus station in Ortonville to see me off. The bus was full, with standing room only. I wasn't about to stand on the bus for 150 miles, so I went back home with them. I told everyone I'd get on the bus the next day.

The next day the bus was also full when the family took me to the bus station, so again I went home with them. The same thing happened the third day. The family was beginning to worry that I might find myself in serious trouble if I didn't return soon, so I finally agreed to get on the bus, even if it was full. Meanwhile, I had received yet another call from my buddy in Sioux Falls, urging me to return. Family pressure prevailed, so I returned to Sioux Falls on the next bus.

October 23, 1945

Dear Mother,

I had been put on orders to report to Major Huber, the assignment officer, last Wednesday morning, but they hadn't marked me AWOL. I told the major yesterday that I missed seeing my name and he said, that's OK, I'm not going to put you to work as you have over 60 points and will be getting out soon. Will have to come out to the base everyday, in case I am on the pre-separation list and need to be processed.

I got a sleeping room in a house in Sioux Falls for Gustie and me. It cost $5.00 per week, with an extra charge of $2.00 if we wanted cooking privileges. Several days later my number did come up and I received my discharge, honorable of course.

Since I was married when I was discharged, I received two Pullman car train tickets to the place where I'd been inducted, Long Beach, California. Gustie really wanted to go to California. She had never done any traveling, but I'd done more than my share of traveling. The last thing I wanted to do was get on a train and go anywhere. I just wanted to get on with my life, which didn't include a trip to California. The tickets never got used (and occasionally Gustie still complains about it).

I had been in the army about 2 ½ years total. It was an experience I'll never forget. I met some of the most wonderful people and saw some of them die in combat. It would take years for most of us to put our experiences into perspective, if ever we could. One thing that we had in common was that we all went on, looking to the future. I had gone to war and, as promised, I had returned home. It has been a good life.

90. Wayne and his mother, Orrilla, after the war ended.

EPILOGUE

He's gone now. Dad died about six weeks after the first printing of this book. Due to his poor health, I'm not sure he understood we completed our project or finished our mission, so to speak. We lost him on October 18, 2001, his 56th wedding anniversary.

I ended the original version of this book by providing updates on some of the main characters in this book, what they had done with their lives after WWII, and where they were living. We've lost so many of them since that time. I won't go there again.

As I read through the story again, I recalled many conversations and informal interviews with Dad, fond memories. There were many like him from that generation of Americans. Profoundly impacted by the Depression, they had no expectation that life would be easy for them, financially or otherwise. Hardship was a way of life. When America was thrust into World War II, these young Americans responded to the call, and they prevailed. They weren't all heroes, at least not in their own minds, but they didn't quit. Even when they couldn't see the end in sight, they continued to work together, and they didn't quit. Perhaps there's a uniqueness in that. It is certainly part of their legacy.

I recall a conversation with Dad that occurred in the early stages of our project. We were having breakfast in our favorite coffee shop when the conversation took place. Several years after WWII he worked in a glass shop in Sioux Falls, South Dakota. He regularly replaced windshields for a nearby car dealership. One of the owners of the dealership was a man named Joe Foss, a WWII Marine pilot and recipient of the Medal of Honor, who later became the governor of South Dakota, among his many accomplishments. Dad told me he knew Joe on a casual basis and saw him quite often. This aroused my curiosity.

I asked Dad if he ever talked to Joe about WWII, since they had both flown in the war. He answered that everyone knew Joe was a war hero, but they never talked of their combat or flying experiences. He said they discussed other things, but the topic of WWII never came up. I asked him if he ever considered why it hadn't come up. Here's his answer, as I remember it. "We had children to raise, bills to pay and mouths to feed. Nearly all of us young men had been in the war." He paused for a second, lost in thought, looked up at me and continued, "Besides, we had already done that."

Yes, Dad, you had already done that. Thank you.

JW

Appendix A

Arthur Lindell's Crew—Still Missing

A shroud of mystery surrounds the crew of Lt. Arthur Lindell. For nearly 60 years the location of the crash site was unknown. None of the nine-man crew returned at the end of the war and they were declared deceased by the Air Force, although circumstances surrounding their deaths were unknown and their remains were not recovered.

The target that day, December 26, 1944, was the Blechhammer South synthetic oil refinery. Lt. Lindell's copilot, Duke Wareham, was replaced on this mission by Avery Gilliland, a pilot who recently arrived in Italy. It was Gilliland's first combat mission, a check ride of sorts, to gain experience before flying with his own crew. One of the gunners, Joseph Lajkowicz, was also not a regular member of Lindell's crew. The plane received a direct hit behind the ball turret, while over the target, just seconds after dropping its bombs. Witnesses in the formation saw the plane break into two pieces, the tail falling separately. No parachutes were seen. At least one airman saw the fuselage of the aircraft strike the ground, followed by a fiery explosion.

On January 9, 1945 the German commandant of Stalag 344, at Lamsdorf, a British POW camp about 40 kilometers from Blechhammer, reported to the International Red Cross that three

91. Lt. Arthur Lindell's crew. Front (L-R) Myron Yaw, gunner; Alex Abramowich, radio operator; Raymond J. Troutman, gunner; Travis Burns, gunner and Michael Papadopoulis, gunner. Back (L-R) Arthur Lindell, pilot; Duke Wareham, copilot; Lloyd Fox, bombardier and Howard Boslow, navigator. (Troutman, Wareham and Fox were not on the crew when they went down.)

92. Avery Gilliland

American airmen were killed in a crash on December 26, 1944 and were buried nearby. Those three airmen were Joseph Lajkowicz, Alex Abramowich and Michael Papadopoulos, all gunners on Lindell's crew. They were listed as Killed in Action. There were no reports about the others on the crew. American reports from that time showed the crash location to be several miles northwest of the refinery.

When the war ended, the Soviets took over control of Poland. The Cold War had started. An American Graves Registration Unit team searched this part of Poland in 1947, making some recoveries and identifications. The crash site of Lindell's plane was not found, nor were the remains of any of the crew found. (At least none of the recoveries were identified as part of this crew.) As diplomatic relations became more strained during the Cold

93. Joseph Lajkowicz

War years, cooperation in MIA issues was nearly non-existent. There is some evidence that the Americans realized in the early 1950's that an expanded search may have produced results, but the doors were closed.

Years went by, while families waited at home, without answers. In the late 1990's Barry Wareham took an interest in the case. Barry's father, Duke Wareham, was the copilot who was saved by fate. Wareham was replaced by Avery Gilliland on the December 26th mission. It didn't seem likely to Barry that the plane, hit and broken into pieces directly over the target, would have landed nearly 30 miles away. Barry brainstormed with Polish researcher Szymon Serwatka, a member of A.M.I.A.P. (Aircraft Missing in Action Project) and together they plotted the course of the group on the mission and came up with a hypothetical crash area, northeast of the target.

In 2001, they enlisted the aid of a local newspaper, which printed an article requesting information about an airplane crash in late December, 1944. Soon there were responses, including one eyewitness account by Jerzy Placzek, a small boy at the time. Local WWII historian Waldemar Ociepski actively sought answers from local residents. Placzek confirmed the crash site for the main fuselage of a B-24. A local mortician confirmed that the remains of five dead airmen were removed from the plane, buried locally, and later removed by the American mission that came through after the war. Further research revealed the tail fell on an abandoned house, with the remains of one crewman inside the plane. The remains of two other airmen were found in the countryside, between the nose and tail, and the body of the last airman was found in a nearby stream in the spring of 1945.

Serwatka located a German report for the crash site identified by Placzek, with the tail serial numbers listed. The numbers matched those of Lindell's plane, so there was no doubt they were on the right track.

Serwatka presented his research information to the Pentagon's DPMO office (Defense Prisoner of War/Missing Personnel Office) for further investigation. A plausible theory is that the remains of at least some of these airmen were recovered in the late 40's when the American Graves Registration Unit came through this area. They were not identified because they were a long distance from where the erroneous records indicated they crashed. Serwatka's research revealed the remains of approximately 60 unidentified American airmen were exhumed from southern Poland after WWII and reburied in an American military cemetery in Western Europe. At this time there has been no match up between any of the unknowns and the nine men from this crew. Many of the Graves Registration Units files are lost or missing and there is currently no way to determine which of the unknowns were recovered from this part of Poland.

In September 2004, the author (Jerry Whiting) visited Blechhammer with his editor, Elliott Dushkin and Bill Williams. Williams, a ball gunner on Avery Gilliland's crew who didn't fly the December 26th mission, promised to visit Blechhammer one day and pay his respects. He finally had the opportunity. Waldemar Ociepski took the men to the crash site, where they

94. Bill Williams, 828th B.S. ball gunner, and eyewitness Jerzy Placzek place flowers at site where Lt. Arthur Lindell's plane crashed on December 26, 1944. (Sept 2004)

were met by Jerzy Placzek, the eyewitness. Placzek related what he saw that day when the plane fell from the sky. The group held a private ceremony, placing a wreath at the crash site. Ociepski assisted the Americans in recovering some small pieces of the aircraft, which were later provided to some of the families of the fallen airmen. Perhaps some day the airmen will be identified and returned.[1]

The 485th Bomb Group flew nine missions to the Blechhammer refineries (north and south). The first mission was July 7, 1944 and the last was the December 26th mission. Nine crews from the group went down on these missions.

NOTES AND REFERENCES

1 The background for this story is from a September 2005 interview with Szymon Serwatka and Barry Wareham in Tucson, Arizona and a document prepared by Szymon Serwatka, for the DPMO , entitled *The research report on the case of Lt. Arthur E. Lindell.*

Appendix B
Red Tail Letter

This is a copy of the actual letter that was left on the radio operator's table of Lt. Baker's plane at Ramitelli.

TO THE VISITING PILOTS AND CREWS:

YOU HAVE BEEN THE GUESTS OF THE 332ND ALL NEGRO FIGHTER GROUP. WE HOPE THAT OUR FACILITIES, SUCH AS THEY ARE, WERE SUITABLE AND ADEQUATE ENOUGH TO HAVE MADE YOUR STAY HERE A PLEASANT ONE. ON BEHALF OF COLONEL DAVIS AND THE COMMAND, I EXTEND TO YOU OUR MOST HEARTY WISHES FOR A HAPPY NEW YEAR AND MANY HAPPIER LANDINGS. YOU ARE WELCOME TO RETURN HERE AT ANY TIME AND I AM SURE THAT WE CAN MAKE YOUR STAY AN ENJOYABLE ONE. THE PILOTS OF THIS COMMAND HAVE EXPRESSED THEIR DESIRES TO HAVE IT MADE CLEAR THAT IT IS A PLEASURE TO BE ABLE TO PROTECT YOU AND LOOK AFTER YOUR WELL-BEING BOTH IN THE AIR AND HERE ON THE GROUND. REMEMBER, WHEN YOU ARE UP THERE AND SEE THE RED TAILED MUSTANGS IN THE SKY, THEY ARE YOUR FRIENDS OF THE 332ND FIGHTER GROUP. HERE IS HOPING FOR A QUICK ENDING OF THE WAR AND A BETTER AND MORE PEACEFUL WORLD.

MANY HAPPY LANDINGS,

D. WEAVER,
Capt., Air Corps,
Public Relations O.

Appendix C

The Tragedy of Ditching

January 20, 1945 was a tragic day for the 485th Bomb Group. Colonel John Tomhave led the formation of 28 bombers to the target. Two aircraft returned early, due to mechanical problems. The group was forced to alter their course twice, after turning onto the bomb run, because of other groups encroaching on their space. These changes forced the group to bomb from a different axis of attack, but the group still made a successful bomb run.

Target photos later revealed approximately 20 bomb strikes in the general target area, with four hits in the specific target area. The group encountered intense, accurate flak of heavy caliber over the target. Fifteen planes had minor damage and five planes received no damage. Twenty planes landed safely back at Venosa. One plane crash-landed at Madna. Two aircraft, low on gas, landed at forward fields (Vis and Ancona). Three aircraft, low on gas, were forced to ditch in the Adriatic Sea. The tragedy of the day lies with those aircraft that were forced to ditch.

The three planes involved were original planes in the group, all having flown overseas when the group was formed. Henry Kogelschatz's crew, an 828th Squadron crew, was flying *Yankee Doodle Dandy*, 42-52718 (Red A). This crew had been in Italy since the previous October and was an experienced crew. They ditched near the island of Andrija, west of Vis. When last heard on the radio, they were on the emergency frequency, just off the coast of Yugoslavia. The entire 9-man crew perished in the ditching.[1]

Another plane that crashed was piloted by John Dobler, 828th Squadron. The crew had only flown one or two missions and had been in Italy about a month. They were flying an 831st Squadron plane, *Valiant Lady*, 42-52699 (Blue S). The plane was low on gas and the crew was trying to make it to the emergency field on the island of Vis. They ran out of gas and were forced to ditch in the Vis harbor, near Lucica. The tail struck the water first and the plane broke in half. Four of the men, all on the flight deck, were thrown clear and survived. The others were killed. The local residents used boats to pick up the four survivors, who were taken to a British field hospital on Vis and later evacuated to Bari by a C-47.[2]

The third plane that ditched was an 830th Squadron plane, piloted by John Biles. The plane, 42-94750, *Pick-Up* (White L), ditched in the Adriatic, off the coast of Italy. The pilot reported from the vicinity of the Yugoslavian coastline that he was low on gas and was having engine trouble. Biles said he was going to attempt to make it to the emergency field at Ancona, Italy. BIG FENCE took a bearing on the aircraft and their location was known. (Author's note: BIG FENCE was the call sign for a VHF radio station, used in emergencies, primarily by damaged planes and planes low on fuel in need of assistance. By having the pilot provide a test count, BIG FENCE operators could home in on the radio signal of the aircraft, identifying the plane's position and provide a "steer" or compass heading to the nearest friendly base or closest friendly territory.) The entire 10-man crew was killed. [3]

There were 29 men on these three aircraft that ditched. Of these 29 men, 25 died from injuries suffered or drowning. The B-24 was a difficult plane to ditch. These losses provided a sad reminder that, although the three aircraft escaped the flak and fighters, the danger was never over until the planes made safe landings back at base. It was a rarity for the 485th to lose three planes and crews on any single mission at this stage of the war.[4]

NOTES AND REFERENCES

1 The crew of Henry Kogelschatz consisted of Robert Ross, copilot; Duwane Eggleston, navigator; Chester Bailey, right waist gunner; George Feany, left waist gunner; Virgil Robertson, nose gunner; Edward Jacobs, top turret gunner; Ray Winslow, ball gunner and Benjamin Weissner, tail gunner.

2 Those who died in the ditching were John Dobler, pilot; Charles Burgess, copilot; Robert Vanderpool, navigator; William Vaughn, gunner; Oliver Robertson, gunner, and Samuel Elliott, gunner. The survivors were Bruno Mininni, bombardier; William Oakley, gunner; Carl Poling, gunner, and Russell Kreps, gunner.

3 In addition to the Biles, the crew consisted of Edward Kapaloski, copilot; Robert Regnier, navigator; Merton Bilsky, bombardier; George Lieblang, radio operator; Bloyce Hargrave, flight engineer; Anderson Garrett, top turret gunner; Calvin Copps, ball gunner; Wesley Giese, nose gunner, and Jack Peters, tail gunner.

4 The sources of information for this story are the Individual Deceased Personnel files (293 files) of Chester Bailey, Robert Vanderpool, and Edward Kapaloski, the 485th BG mission report for 1/20/45 and the combined Escape Statement for Bruno Mininni, Carl Poling, Russell Kreps and William Oakley.

Photo List and Credits

51. Officers in mud . . . . Jim Scheib

52. Lt. Phil Stone. . . . . Smoky Harsh family

53. Lt. Stone in hospital . . . . Phil Stone

54. Ken Wydler's crew . . . . Robert Espenshade family

55. Wydler's plane . . . . Robert Espenshade family

56. David Blood . . . . John Beck

57. Lew Baker . . . . John Beck

58. George Benedict . . . . Eugene McCarthy family

59. Eugene Cogburn. . . . . Eugene McCarthy family

60. Captain James Johnson . . . . . 485th Bomb Group archives

61. Tom Tamraz . . . . Tom Tamraz family

62. Fred Sherer . . . . Jeanne Sherer Gogolski

63. Warren LaFrance . . . . Hal Wilder

64. Partisans with Blood's crew . . . . . Jeanne Sherer Gogolski

65. Colonel Tomhave in plane . . . 485th Bomb Group archives

66. Major Olen Cooper Bryant . . . . Cooper Bryant family

66a. Lt. Carl Stockdale's crew . . . . Earl Beatty

67. Walter Fergus . . . . 485th Bomb Group archives

68. Roy Burke . . . . 485th Bomb Group archives

68a Luigi Naidon . . . . Enzo Vinci/Fabio Stergulc

68b Father Giovanni Lenarduzzi . . . Enzo Vinci/Fabio Stergulc

69. Lt. Colonel John Atkinson . . . . 485th Bomb Group archives

70. Glen Warden crew . . . . 485th Bomb Group archives

71. Capri sightseeing. . . . . John Manfrida family

72. Wayne at Capri . . . . Whiting family collection

73. Col Cornett with Acheson and Twining . 485th Bomb Group

74. B.W. Nauman with girls . . . . . . Whiting family collection

75. Gerald Morris . . . . Diane Morris Leslie

76. Dick Fedell and Walter Michalke . . . . . . Walter Michalke

BIBLIOGRAPHY

Baker, Robert. *Tail Heavy* (a personal memoir). Hickory Corners, Michigan: Private printing.

Birdsall, Steve. *Log of the Liberators.* New York: Doubleday, 1973

Freeman, Roger. *B-24 Liberator at War.* London England: Ian Allan, 1983.

Holway, John B. *Red Tails, Black Wings: The Men of America's Black Air Force.* Las Cruces, New Mexico: Yucca Tree Press, 1997.

Kempffer, Harold J. *As I Remember* (a personal memoir). Apple Valley, Minnesota: Private printing, revised edition 2002.

Lindsay, Franklin. *Beacons in the Night: With the OSS and Tito's Partisans in Wartime Yugoslavia.* Stanford, California: Stanford University Press, 1993.

Miller, Francis Trevelyan. *The Complete History of WWII.* Chicago, Illinois: Readers Service Bureau, 1947.

Rust, Kenn C. *Fifteenth Air Force Story.* Temple City, California: Historical Aviation Album, 1976.

Schneider, Sammy. *This Is How It Was.* St. Petersburg, Florida: Southern Heritage Press, 1995.

Schneider, Sammy. *Missions by the Numbers.* Littleton, Colorado: Private Printing

Selhaus, Edi. *Evasion and Repatriation: Slovene Partisans and the Rescued American Airmen in WWII.* Manhattan, Kansas: Sunflower University Press, 1993.

Serwatka, Szymon (Mucha, Michal and Kassak, Peter). *Z Ziemi Wloskiej Do Polskiej.* Poland: Biuro Uslug Komputerowych –Stanislaw Smaga, 2003.

Whiting, Jerry. *Don't Let The Blue Star Turn Gold: Downed Airmen in Europe in WWII.* Walnut Creek, California: Tarnaby Books, 2005.

Wilder, Harold Jr. *Grandfather Stories:* Camarillo, California: Hayes Graphics, 2002

INDEX

C

M

The Author

Jerry Whiting is a South Dakota native and a graduate of the University of California, Santa Barbara, with a Bachelor of Arts degree. He later earned a Masters Degree at John F. Kennedy University.

Jerry worked in Law Enforcement for 28 years in the San Francisco Bay Area, holding a variety of positions. During his unique career he had an opportunity to work with police departments in several European countries, studying tactics and procedures and spent a brief period as an observer with the Cheyenne River Sioux Tribal Police in South Dakota.

He has written two other books about World War II. *Don't Let the Blue Star Gold: Downed Airmen in Europe in WWII* is a series of stories about American bomber crews shot down over occupied Europe and focuses on their fates after they were shot down. His other book in print is *Veterans in the Mist: World War II Memoirs of the Third Thursday Lunch Bunch.* This is a book about a group of World War II Vets who live near him and meet monthly to share memories. This book contains personal accounts of the experiences of more than 20 these men, from the jungles of New Guinea to the Ardennes Forest, and beyond. He travelled extensively to research the stories for his books.

In addition, he recently produced a 24-minute documentary entitled *In the Shadow of Mt. Vulture; Venosa Then and Now*. This film is about 15th Air Force airmen stationed at a base in Italy and answers the question of whether their efforts and sacrifice are still remembered today in the region.

The author regularly assists other researchers here and abroad. He has consulted with and provided training for the Dept. of Defense (DPMO) on MIA issues. He is currently the Historian for the 485th Bomb Group Association and served as publisher for their group history, *Missions by the Numbers: combat Missions Flown by the 485th Bomb Group (H).* Jerry has written articles for periodicals and magazines and is often called upon as a guest speaker, where he always emphasizes the importance of preserving our rich American history and the lessons to be learned from it. He teaches part-time and he and his wife live in Walnut Creek, California.

You may contact the author directly for signed copies of books or with questions or comments at EAJWWhiting @aol.com. You can read more about his books on his website at: www. jwhitingwarstories.com

43332546R00149

Made in the USA
Middletown, DE
06 May 2017